Other Books by Gary Richmond

A View from the Zoo
The Divorce Decision
Please Don't Feed the Bears

ALL GOD'S CREATURES

GARY RICHMOND

WORD PUBLISHING
Dallas · London · Vancouver · Melbourne

All God's Creatures

Unless noted otherwise, Scripture quotations are from The Holy Bible, New International Version (NIV). Copyright © 1973, 1978, 1984 International Bible Society. Used by permission of Zondervan Bible Publishers.

Other Scripture quotations are from the following sources:

Those identified as KJV are from the King James Version.

Those marked NASB are from The New American Standard Bible, © The Lockman Foundation 1960, 1962, 1963, 1968, 1971, 1972, 1973, 1975, 1977.

Those marked NRSV are from The New Revised Standard Version Bible, copyrighted 1989 by the Division of Christian Education of the National Council of the Churches of Christ in the U.S.A., and are used by permission.

Those marked RSV are from The Revised Standard Version of the Bible, copyrighted 1946, 1952, © 1971, 1973 by the Division of Christian Education of the National Council of the Churches of Christ in the U.S.A., and are used by permission.

Those marked TLB are from The Living Bible, copyright 1971 by Tyndale House Publishers, Wheaton, Ill. Used by permission.

Library of Congress Cataloging-in-Publication Data:

Richmond, Gary. 1944–
    All God's creatures : spiritual lessons from the animals of the
Bible / Gary Richmond.
        p.   cm.
    ISBN 0–8499–3251–3
    1. Animals in the Bible.   2. Animals—Religious aspects—
Christianity.   I.   Title.
    BS663.R53   1991
    220.8'591—dc20   91–35668
                                                              CIP

 2 3 4 9   LB   9 8 7 6 5 4 3 2
Printed in the United States of America

To Lorraine Austin

for making me love the Bible in a way that no one else has. You made me want to take a closer look for myself. You are and remain the teacher's teacher. Thank you!

To Jack Badal

for making me understand that caring for animals was an art, a noble pursuit. You made me take a closer look at the creatures God has made. Life has been richer and more fascinating because of what you have shown me. Thank You!

Contents

Introduction

I was always the little boy outside everyone's windows calling out, "Ya wanna come out an' play? It's too nice to stay inside." With a nature like that, it takes more than a little to get me to sit down with paper and pen, touch a typewriter, or turn on a word processor and spend a few hundred hours researching, arranging words, and spell checking. I have to believe that something I might write will help someone, that someone would better understand or be encouraged by something I can say. I also have to be convinced that someone else hasn't already found a better way to say what I have to say. If what I want to say has already been said, then I can spend my time with the people I enjoy playing and talking with, especially my wife Carol and our children, their spouses, and our grandchildren. If you're a people person and also a little hyper on the side, writing is fun and torture all at the same time. Writing goes a little against my grain, but I'm thankful for the opportunity and will continue to write as long as someone wants and needs to read what I have to say.

So why did I write this book?

I was an animal keeper and a veterinary assistant for seven years at the Los Angeles Zoo, which is the fifth largest zoo in the world. During that time, I met some of the most knowledgeable people in the animal world. I worked with Drs. Charles Sedgewick and Jonathan Bernstein, two of the finest zoo veterinarians in the world. Dale Thompson, my best friend, is considered to be one of the best bird experts in the world. Harvey Fisher, the zoo's renowned curator of reptiles, was always available to fill me in on the creatures under his care, and he's still willing to answer every question I can dream up about these scaly friends. I met Jack Badal, the world's foremost animal keeper and a legendary trainer among his peers. He always answered my questions, although he delighted in making me figure them out for myself. Thus, for a short time, I was privileged to live in a world of mystical and awesomely savage beauty with others who understood the task of keeping and caring for animals.

For twenty-two years, I have served as camp naturalist and Father Nature to the Forest Home Christian Conference Center. There, I was allowed to walk the trails with Clarence Zylstra, the most well-rounded naturalist I know.

In short, I have been exposed firsthand to the world of Creation that most people never see or begin to understand during the whole of their lifetime. It wasn't so long ago that ours was an agricultural society. Then almost everyone knew something about farm animals and crops, but today we are for the most part city dwellers, part of a new wilderness. Our concept of an encounter with nature is setting out roach traps or dipping the family dog as a measure of flea control. There is no room in our life for critters. Our gardens are small patches of green growth, and we are bent on removing the healthy indigenous plants that invade them (namely, weeds). We are city-fied.

This trend, however, has generated a gap in our understanding of nature and its influence on our lives. This has also affected our understanding of several Bible passages. The Bible was written by people who spent their lives outdoors and who survived by learning from the Creation generated by God. When you think about it, you see that Moses spent at least 80 of his 120 years in the great outdoors. Forty of those years were spent with sheep. During that time, he saw lions, bears, cobras, and scorpions; he saw almost every creature that ever flew, crawled, or walked. He learned from them what the Lord wanted him to learn. So when he wrote, he naturally included illustrations from his exposure and imagined that anyone who read what he had written would naturally understand. For some thirty-five centuries or so, he was right. But today, few of us are farmers or herdsmen. So much of the Bible gets past us. We don't see what it has to say, because we don't know where to look.

Preachers used to be the sons of farmers, and so they were able to bring some of the original flavor of the biblical text to their listeners. Today, they're the sons of engineers, insurance salesmen, and building contractors. They drive to church and to visit their constituents on paved roads, and the closest they get to nature are the road kills that occasionally litter the roadside. They too have become city dwellers, because they minister to a flock of city dwellers. When they come across a wonderful nature story in the Bible, they don't have the background to appreciate it. Most of the reference books to which they can refer have been written by people more deskbound than they.

During my years with the zoo and the conference center, scripture passage after scripture passage has come alive with the lessons drawn from nature and the animal kingdom. They cannot be understood without the perspective of a naturalist. For example, when Jesus told his followers to be as wise as serpents, what did he mean? Serpents make us think of Satan. It doesn't fit. But I have heard many teachers and preachers say that Jesus is saying that we should be like Satan, meaning that we should be able to fight fire with fire or that we should at least be as good at something as Satan is. But Jesus wouldn't want that. He didn't mean Satan; he meant snakes. He created them, and there are things about snakes that are very wise. You'll find them in the chapter on snakes.

Peter tells us that Satan prowls around the earth like a roaring lion. As frightful as that passage is, there's more to it when you know why a lion roars. You'll find that out in the chapter on lions.

There's a biblical passage similar to our expression "out of the frying pan, into the fire." It's in the chapter on bears.

I probably wouldn't have written this book had I not heard one of my favorite preachers misfire while

---

teaching from the story of Elijah being fed by the ravens. Most preachers interpret this story as the Lord's giving his prophet a little rest and relaxation. Their word pictures hit my mind in Disney-scope as the wistful little birds flew to the prophet of the Lord with bunches of food and sustenance. You'll see what it really means in the chapter on ravens.

The bottom line is that knowing a little about what may be behind a passage or a reference is fascinating. I want to share that with you, so you'll appreciate these animal passages as much as I do. "Ya wanna come out an' play?" Join me on this safari through Scripture.

Gary Richmond

1

LIONS

THERE IS AN ODDITY AMONG ZOO KEEPERS that I believe is unique to our profession: While on vacation we like to visit other zoos. Most people like to get away from what they normally do. But we like to interact with exotic animals and see the inner workings of other zoos. I did every time I got the chance.

One summer, while vacationing in Southern California, I took the opportunity to visit the small and immaculate zoo in San Jose. One of the exhibits that caught my interest was that of the large cats, which of course included lions. The zoo's director, Don Bracken, had departed radically from standard zoo philosophy by exhibiting only *tamed* cats. Ordinarily, taming wild animals is avoided because, as the old-timers had taught us, "It's the tame ones that get you!"—a saying that has been proven true throughout zoo histories. Incidents involving the death of zoo personnel have almost always been attributable to keepers trusting animals that were supposedly tame. We tend to forget that a wild animal, fourteen to twenty-one times stronger than a man (which would be true of both lions and tigers), can have a bad day, regardless of whether it's tame or not.

Despite my knowing all this, I surprised myself by asking Don if I might be allowed to enter the African lion cage at his zoo. You see, the Los Angeles Zoo operated within the counsel of the wise. We had no tame lions with whom we might play. So I thought if I were ever going to have the experience of socializing with the king of beasts, this would probably be my only chance. The question popped out of my mouth before I had time to consider the consequences. What was more amazing than my question was the fact that Don, with a sly smile and a just noticeable twinkle in his eye, said, "Sure, glad to oblige you."

With me was my wife Carol, our children, my wife's sister Darla, and her children. I sensed in Carol a certain wifely lack of enthusiasm for my adventure. Darla asked Carol if my going in with the lions bothered her. She answered yes. She thought that I was clearly showing a lack of wisdom and maturity by allowing myself to be torn apart by lions in front of my children, wife, and relatives. She had a point. But I was an experience collector, and taking this experience back to my zoo would be a trophy too great to pass up.

Don and I made small talk as we walked to the cage together.

"The female is a sweetheart; you'll love her. She can't get enough attention," said Don, as he fumbled for his keys.

"What about the male?" I probed.

"Moody."

"Moody?"

4

"Good days and bad days. You know how it is."

I didn't know how it was, but I nodded as if I did.

As we entered the cage, I kept my eye on the regal male who was laying on the sleeping bench next to his mate. The bench stood about four feet off the ground. He stared at me, looking directly into my eyes for several seconds. His green eyes were alert but emotionless. At the same moment that he looked away, his ears went down and his tail began to twitch nervously. He was in a mood.

"He's in a mood, isn't he, Don?"

"Believe so. Wouldn't be good to push him, I think."

"Push him?"

"Maybe it would be best just to leave him be."

"Should we step out?" I asked sincerely.

"The female's fine. We'll just spend a little time with her," he answered coolly.

"He doesn't mind if I pet the female, does he?"

"Never has before. We'll just keep an eye on him."

(Why did I feel like I was playing "You Bet Your Life?")

As I approached, the female rolled over to be petted. Her 270-pound frame was about average size for a female. She stared lovingly, and I reached up and scratched her neck just behind the ear. She looked as if she were in ecstasy. She generated the lion equivalent of a purr, which, at about fifty times the intensity of a cat's purring, was a little disturbing. The male, who was just three feet away, glanced at me, turned away again, and growled. The growl, clearly distinguishable from the purr, raised my level of concern another notch. I looked back at Don, but he didn't seem concerned, so I stayed by the female's side, rubbed her stomach, and talked quietly to her.

"Rubbing her tummy makes her playful," Don warned. He was right. In a moment, she stood up on her bench and stretched. That stance revealed all of her usually concealed claws. They were long and very capable of turning anything into shredded wheat. Then she yawned, exposing massive muscular jaws and long, deadly canines. She jumped off of the bench and rubbed against my legs affectionately, whereupon I vigorously scratched her back. I was confronting death, showing off in front of family and relatives, and mentally recording an experience that most of my peers at the L.A. Zoo would never be able to duplicate. There was also a sense of mastery over a savage beast, the sense that this awesome predator was subjecting itself to a superior.

Boy, did all that change quickly!

The female walked about ten feet away from me and turned. She looked at me playfully, and then she bounced my way. She leaped up and grasped me around the chest. She squeezed very tightly, forcing all the air from my lungs. My arms were pinned beneath her firm grip; I couldn't move them. I have never felt more helpless in my life. Her "play" strength was beyond my wildest imagination. As we stood there in a waltz position, it was obvious to me that she and I had two distinctly different desires. She wanted to play and I wanted to breathe. I turned to Don, who was smiling. He had that so-you-wanted-to-play-with-a-lion look (translation: "I told you so!").

"Don, she's playing a little rough," I said.

Literally, I felt as though I were in a vise, an immovable vise. I was beginning to panic; only pride kept me from losing my dignity. And, although the thought did occur to me, whimpering just didn't seem appropriate.

Don stepped forward and yelled, "Down, girl!" and hit her squarely on the head with the palm of his hand. He hit her hard, because the blow pulled me down a bit before she let go.

"Don't make her mad," I blurted out, as I glanced at the male lion to see how he was feeling about the whole thing. His tail was twitching more than ever, and he was staring back and forth between Don and me. He didn't look like he would have taken that sort of blow from a mere human, and I was glad when Don said, "Hey, we have a tame jaguar named Christopher. Let me take you to his cage. . . . He's a real sweetheart."

I left that cage a different man. For one thing, there was no more adrenaline in my adrenal glands. I was drained completely of energy. But more than that, I had a realistic view of lions. Before the lioness hugged me, I saw lions as cartoons, fantasy playthings, the Hollywood image. In every old-time jungle movie ever made, the hero slays the ferocious lion, thus saving the life of his lady fair. The poor helpless lion, at the mercy of the hero's courage, strength, and stamina, never had a chance. Now I know for certain that those scenes were well choreographed. Lions are much more animal than I ever dreamed. Unless you have *felt* that kind of strength, I know it's difficult to imagine, . . . just take my word for it.

At the same time, my up-close-and-personal experience caused an interesting thing to happen. Scriptures that included lions absolutely came alive for me. My newfound respect offered me a realistic perspective from which to view the writers' analogies. The first verses to come to mind for me were 1 Peter 5:8–9:

> Be sober, be watchful. Your adversary the devil prowls around like a roaring lion, seeking some one to devour. Resist him, firm in your faith, knowing that the same experience of suffering is required of your brotherhood throughout the world.

The phrase "a roaring lion" or "a lion roared" comes up here and many other times in Scripture, so it is important to know something about what a roar is or means. When this passage says that "the devil prowls around like a roaring lion," we need to know something about roaring so that we can learn what the verse has to teach us.

A lion's roar may be heard over a distance of nearly five miles. The sound of the roar registers somewhere between 1 and 3 kHz. (The deepest bass gospel singer never dreamed of singing that loud without blowing every vocal cord in his larynx.) The roar is so loud and so low that if a lion were to roar near you, it would literally vibrate through your whole body.

So we know that its roar is loud and powerful, but what does it mean and what does it have to do with Satan? Well, every reason for a lion to roar relates in some way to Satan's methodology. Lions do most of their roaring at night, under the cover of darkness. Darkness is where Satan does his best work. Did you know that three o'clock in the morning is generally referred to as the "soul's midnight," because most people die in hospitals at about that time? Satan loves death, the pain it causes, and the faith it assaults. The majority of violent crimes, robberies, and rapes occur after the sun has fled the western sky. The Bible says it clearly, "Men loved darkness rather than light, because their deeds were evil" (John 3:19 RSV). Did you ever hear of a witches' coven or a satanic movement that called a meeting at twelve noon in an open field? Never. The occult meets at night. Do you remember the saying, "It's always darkest before the dawn?" Lions most often roar before the dawn, between three and six o'clock in the morning. That leads to the first and primary reason that lions roar.

Reason 1: Lions roar to create fear—paralyzing, heart-stopping, soul-wrenching, immobilizing fear. When they attack their prey, most of which is pretty easily frightened anyway, they gain that much more of an advantage by roaring as they attack.

Satan's best tool is fear. Jesus knew that, and that's why He and the angels are forever saying, "Fear not." We are his sheep, and lions attack sheep. But the Lord is our Shepherd. And remember, "Greater is He that is in you than he that is in the world."

Reason 2: Lions roar to gather their pride (their family). It is their way of saying, "Here I am."

Any speech delivered by Adolf Hitler, Fidel Castro, or Saddam Hussein is the evil lion saying, "Here I am." Any magazine stand selling *Penthouse*, *Playboy*, or any other woman-exploiting trash is Satan calling out, "Here I am."

Reason 3: Lions roar to herald their territory. The roar is hostile and says, "You will pay dearly if you try to take this territory away from me." An animal's territory is what it is most likely willing to die for. We can understand that, for we have given many of our fathers, brothers, and sons up in battle to protect our land. We stand ready to do it again.

Satan, once he has claimed any territory, is savage about keeping it. He had claimed the Auca Indians in South America; they belonged to him. Jim Elliot was killed trying to claim the Aucas for the Lord Jesus. Did God not protect Jim? Yes and no. He offered Jim a crack at God's highest calling, and Jim took it. Then, as his reward, God took Jim through the gates of splendor. Satan won no victory over a man who demonstrated this highest calling. Jesus said, "Greater love has no man than this. That he should lay down his life for his friend."

Reason 4: Lions use their roar to intimidate their competitors. They run off other lions or leopards that might compete for prey.

That compares with Satan's convincing us that someone is beyond our help, too far gone. That's when he says that you'll be hurt if you get involved; you'll be arrested or sued if you try to help.

I can truthfully say that I was afraid of the devil before, but now I realize that when the devil "prowls around like a roaring lion, seeking some one to devour," I do *not* want to be the one he seeks.

In a wonderful book by the famous African missionary Robert Moffat, there are some fascinating observations that further the parallel between the devil and a roaring lion. In *Missionary Labours and Scenes in Southern Africa,* Moffat described how a lion would manage to mount the back of a giraffe and, with the aid of his sharp claws, rip into the animal's shoulders and gnaw away the flesh until the vertebrae of the neck was exposed. He tenaciously and cruelly persists until he has killed his prey, and then he consumes it. (A lion can eat 30 percent of its own body weight at one sitting. That would be similar to a 150-pound man eating about two hundred Big Macs.) When the lion is successful in his attack on the giraffe, both animals fall and in many instances the lion is lamed for his trouble. Sometimes, if the giraffe is very strong, the victim might succeed in bringing his rider to the ground in time to escape with his life. Although his wounds will eventually heal, he will forever carry the marks of the lion's teeth and claws.

Of course, in the controlled environment of a modern zoo, the chance of a serious hunter/hunted incident, such as the one described by Moffat, are extremely remote. Of all things, it is expected that zoo keepers will protect the animals from each other.

One morning, however, my shift was tested as most zoo keepers haven't been. We were enjoying a mid-morning break when suddenly a mule deer bounded by us. She saw us, turned away, and jumped the fence, clearing it with ease—but she landed in the moat that separated the lions from the viewing public.

As luck would have it, the lions were out, each one roaring in response to the excitement and hungrily watching the terrified doe swim back and forth in the six-foot-deep water.

The deer saw the lions and knew she could not swim in their direction, but the walls around her offered her no footing; they were sheer uprights. Her choices were limited. On one side were the roaring lions and on the other were the keepers calling and yelling for her to keep swimming until some equipment and additional help could get there.

Finally, the veterinarian came on the scene with some rope and a couple of pieces of equipment called "come alongs." You know what rope looks like, but a "come along" is a strong aluminum pole with a noose at one end that can be tightened like a collar after it has been slipped over an animal's head.

Three ropes were handed to the keepers who claimed to have some roping skill. The two "come alongs" were given to the other men who were skilled at capturing animals.

The frightened doe only recognized that she faced danger on both sides, and she instinctively fought all our attempts to help her. In truth, none of the keepers were very skilled at roping, so continued efforts appeared futile. Even when a rope finally did circle her head, she just dipped under the water and left it floating on the surface.

We soon realized that she was tiring from her continuous swimming. Her body was lower in the water, and her breathing was labored. We were clearly loosing the race to time. The look in her eyes was no longer sharp; she was becoming disoriented and exhausted. She began to circle, swimming in a dream-like fashion—and passing close by the lions who were straining to reach her and pull her to her death. They roared loudly at her, which seemed to snap her out of her dream state, and once again she swam to the middle of the pool. By now she was riding dangerously low in the pool and gasping for breath.

One of the keepers, frustrated by our failure, simply reacted. Without asking or waiting for permission, he dove into the pool and swam to the deer, who was oblivious to his presence by this time. He yelled, "Throw me a rope!" A lasso sailed through the air, landing just within his reach. He looped it over the doe's delicate neck and commanded, "Pull!" The keeper holding the other end of the rope pulled, tightening the noose and turning her body back in the right direction, away from the lions.

The lions were going crazy now, roaring and pacing back and forth. It would not have been out of the ordinary for them to have launched into the moat to attack the deer. Fortunately, that day, they didn't. Most likely, they weren't hungry or the results may have been very different.

The doe was guided to the side of the pool and pulled from the water. The men handling the rope were reluctant to pull at first, afraid that they might accidentally strangle her in the process. Nonetheless, the noose tightened, closing tightly around the doe's neck. For just a moment she was unable to breathe as she was hoisted from the moat. When she was safely out of the water and breathing again, everyone relaxed.

Thankfully, the lions went on about their business, and the danger passed. But during those agonizing moments of helplessness, the mule deer was a sure target. The lions had paced and stalked, waiting patiently (and loudly) for an opportunity to claim the young deer. Then, in the nick of time, she was pulled to safety by a power greater than her own.

And we know the devil to be like those persistent, stalking lions. He patiently waits for just the right moment to claim our lives. The Bible has many things to say about our tenacious adversary. Jesus tells us in John 8:44 that the devil is a murderer; he has been that way from the beginning. He is a predator, feeling nothing for his prey. He is without conscience, remorseless, and focused on two things: deception and murder. He tries in hundreds of ways to get his claws into us and drag us down. He waits for our moment of weakness and searches for our vulnerabilities. Although the Scripture does not guarantee that we will be spared from attack or injury, it offers instead a promise that in Christ we will have victory. Remember 1 Peter 5:9? "Resist him [the devil], firm in your faith, knowing that the same experience of suffering is required of your brotherhood throughout the world." Then in verse 10, "And after you have suffered a little while, the God of all grace, who has called you to his eternal glory in Christ, will himself restore, establish, and strengthen you."

When we who have trusted Christ go to heaven, we, like Moffat's giraffes, will carry with us the scars of our attacker, the evil lion, the devil.

I think of Job. I imagine he could show us a few scars. He was a very wealthy man, the father of many children. He was well liked and respected in his community, and he had many friends. Then one day, the devil took everything from him. He lost ten children. His friends became enemies. He lost his health and suffered physical discomforts. He was really hurting. He was weak and vulnerable, but God pulled him from the moat of despair and hopelessness.

Another personality in our history, and perhaps the most famous missionary of all, is Dr. David Livingston (I presume). In his autobiography, *Livingston's Travels and Researches in South Africa,* he records the most famous incident in his life—when he was attacked by an adult male lion. This story is a literal picture of what will happen to all of us who have trusted Christ with our lives. We will all be attacked by the evil lion, the devil, and we will live with the scars.

At first Livingston was reluctant to tell the story of the lion's attack, because whenever he was able to visit England on furloughs, he was forced to spend more time reliving this event than any other. He considered many other experiences to be of far greater consequence in the building of God's kingdom. He told the story this way:

The Bakatla of the village of Mabotsa were much troubled by lions, which leapt into cattle-pens by night, and destroyed their cows. They even attacked their herds in open day. This was so unusual an occurrence that the people believed that they were bewitched—"given," as they said, "into the power of the lions by a neighboring tribe." They went once to attack the animals, but being a rather cowardly people compared to the Bechuanas in general on such occasions, they returned without killing any.

It is well known that if one of a troup of lions is killed, the others take the hint and leave that part of the country. So, the next time the herds were attacked, I went with the people, in order to encourage them to rid themselves of the annoyance by destroying one of the marauders. We found the lions on a small hill about a quarter of a mile in length, covered with trees.

16

A circle of men was formed round it, and they gradually closed up, ascending pretty close to each other. Being down below on the plain with a native schoolmaster, named Mabalwe, a most excellent man, I saw one of the lions sitting on a piece of rock within the now closed circle of men. Mebalwe fired at him before I could, and the ball struck the rock on which the animal was sitting. He bit at the spot struck, as a dog does at a stick or stone thrown at him; then leaping away, broke through the opening circle and escaped unhurt. The men were afraid to attack him, perhaps on account of their beliefs in witchcraft. When the circle was reformed, we saw two other lions in it; but we were afraid to fire lest we should strike the men, and they allowed the beasts to burst through also. If the Bakatla had acted in the custom of the country, they would have speared the lions in their attempt to get out. Seeing we could not get them to kill one of the lions, we bent our footsteps toward the village; in going around the end of the hill, however, I saw one of the beasts sitting on a piece of rock as before, but this time he had a little bush in front. Being about thirty yards off, I took good aim at his body through the bush, and fired both barrels into it. The man then called out, "He is shot, he is shot!" Others cried, "He has been shot by another man too; let us go to him." I did not see anyone else shoot at him, but I saw the lion's tail erected in anger behind the bush, and turning to the people, said, "Stop a little, till I load again." When in the act of ramming down the bullets I heard a shout. Starting, and looking half round, I saw the lion in the act of springing upon me. I was upon a little height; he caught my shoulder as he sprang, and we both came to the ground below together. Growling horribly close to my ear, he shook me as a terrier dog does a rat. The shock produced a stupor similar to that which seems to be felt by a mouse after the first shake of a cat. It caused a sort of dreaminess, in which there was no sense of pain nor feeling of terror, though quite conscious of all that was happening. It was like what patients partially under the influence of chloroform describe, who see all the operation, but feel not the knife. This singular condition was not the result of any mental process. The shake annihilated fear, and allowed no sense of horror in looking round at the beast. This peculiar state is produced in all animals killed by the carnivore; and if so, is a merciful provision by our benevolent Creator for lessening the pain of death. Turning round to relieve myself of the weight, as he had one paw on the back of my head, I saw his eyes directed to Mebalwe, who was trying to shoot him at a distance of fifteen yards. His gun, a flint one, misfired in both barrels; the lion immediately left me, and attacking Mebalwe, bit his thigh. Another man, whose life I had saved before, after he had been tossed by a buffalo, attempted to spear the lion while he was biting Mebalwe. He left Mebalwe and caught this man by the shoulder, but at that moment the bullets he had received took effect, and he fell down dead. The whole was a work of a few moments, and must have been his paroxysms of dying rage. In order to take the charm from him, the Bakatla on the following day made a huge bonfire over the carcass, which was declared to be that of the largest lion they had ever seen. Besides crunching the bone into splinters, he left eleven teeth wounds on the upper part of my arm.

A wound from this animal's tooth resembles a gunshot wound; it is generally followed by a great deal of sloughing and discharge, and pains are felt in the part periodically ever afterward. I had on a tartan jacket on the occasion, and I believe that it wiped off all the virus from the teeth that pierced the flesh, for my two companions in this affray have both suffered from the peculiar pains, while I have escaped with only the inconvenience of a false joint in my limb. The man whose shoulder was wounded showed me his wound actually burst forth afresh on the same month of the following year. This curious point deserves attention.

Even the great David Livingston bore the scars from his encounter with a lion for most of his life. What an incredible exposition of 1 Peter 5:8–11. It happened as Livingston served the very people God had called him to serve. Can we expect to be spared? I think not. But like Livingston, we will be "established, strengthened, and restored." Did you pick up that the lion in Livingston's story did all of his damage while he was dying?

There is another story which, more than any other, establishes the truth that lions are tenacious and focused on their tasks. *Man-Eaters of Tsavo*, by Colonel J. H. Patterson, tells of the author's encounter with the fierceness of two lions.

Colonel Patterson was a British engineer sent to assist in the building of the Ugandan Railroad. The railroad had penetrated hundreds of miles of veldt and jungle, all of which was alive with hostile tribes, who, like the American Indians, resented the presumption that their land was up for grabs. That's not all—it was also filled with exotic and life-claiming diseases and animals of unimagined numbers and species. Some of the animals were killers, none more famous than lions. It took men with true grit to work at this task, and Patterson seemed to be one of them. He dealt with two man-eating lions that had terrorized thousands of workers and literally brought the railroad to a standstill during a nine-month period.

Tsavo stands midpoint between Mombasa and Nairobi, some one hundred miles from the Indian Ocean. There are many rivers in and about Tsavo, and the surrounding vegetation is so dense that travelers had to crawl on their hands and knees to get through it. I should add that while all these things were true in March 1898, when the man-eaters of Tsavo were establishing their reign of terror, Africa is today as ecologically depleted as the United States, and lions are found mostly in national parks.

Man-eating behavior is not the normal behavior of lions. There is usually a reason why a lion, or in this case two lions out of the hundreds in the area, became exclusively man-eaters. My best guess is that the game hunters, who satisfied the food needs of the thousands of workmen building the railroad, probably put a significant dent in the normal food supply of the lions, so they began to eat the easiest prey left in the neighborhood; namely, humans. Usually, only the elderly or sick lions turn to man killing.

It was not long after Patterson joined the railroad in Tsavo that the first reports of workers being lost to lions came to him. The following is the account of the first incident. It came through the quaint style of a workman who had emigrated from India to build the railroad.

"Sahib," he said, "I was awake and lying next to Ungan Singh, who was fast asleep. I was looking into the moonlight when suddenly I saw a big lion put his head in at the open door. My heart turned to water when I saw him so near me and I could not move. His eyes glowed like coals of fire as he looked first at me and then at Ungan Singh. I almost died of fright lest he should choose me; then, by the kindness of Allah, he seized the jemadar [foreman] by the throat instead of your slave." He went on to relate how the unfortunate foreman called out, "Choro" (let go), and threw his arms up around the lion's neck, but the brute lifted him off of the bed and pulled him away while his terrified companion—wide awake now—lay helpless and panic-stricken, listening to the terrible struggle taking place outside the tent door. Poor Ungan Singh must have died hard, but what chance had he? As the workman gravely remarked later in the report, "Was he not fighting with a lion?"

That was the beginning of the nightmare, and it took Patterson nine months to track down and dispatch the two lions who killed night after terror-filled night. Not long after the lions began to snatch the workmen, one by one, from their tents, the building of the railroad stopped and the work force was used to gather literally tons of branches from thorn-bearing trees and bushes. These branches and bushes were woven together and made into eight- and nine-foot fences, five and six feet thick around their tents and sleeping quarters. The thorny fence was called a boma. This would normally deter the man-eaters and protect the workers during the long fear-ridden nights. It should have, but it didn't.

According to Colonel Patterson, "Alas, this peaceful life was not destined to continue and we were shaken rudely out of our false feeling of security. One night the familiar terror stricken cries and screams rang out once more through the camps, and we knew that the 'demons' had returned and added yet another victim to their long list."

On that occasion, believing that the man-eaters had gone for good, a number of men slept outside their tents beside a campfire, but within the shelter of the thick boma. Suddenly, in the middle of the night, one of the lions was heard forcing his way through the bushes. The alarm was sounded, and sticks, stones, and firebrands were hurled at the stalking intruder, all in an effort to drive him back. None of this, however, was effective, because the lion soon penetrated the thick thorn fence, utterly indifferent to the shrieks and howls of his would-be victims.

When the lions were finally killed, they were both covered with horrible scars from the many times they had forced their way through the bomas. I would call that tenacious, wouldn't you? Listen to Moses, under the inspiration of God:

> Behold, a people! As a lioness it rises up
> and as a lion it lifts itself;
> it does not lie down till it devours the prey,
> and drinks the blood of the slain.

> *Numbers 23:24 RSV*

Does that remind you of Patterson's lions? Tenacious can be a good and bad quality, because it is a trait that can be applied for good or for evil. The passage above is telling Israel what God will be like to them if they stray from His will and protection. You see, the Scripture not only uses the lion as a symbol for the evil one but also for the righteous one.

Of the more than 140 lion passages in the Bible, each one teaches some wonderful things about God, about nature, and about lions. For instance, David was a great naturalist; it is reflected in many of the psalms.

> O LORD my God, in thee do I take refuge;
> save me from all my pursuers, and deliver
> me,
> lest like a lion they rend me,
> dragging me away, with none to rescue.

> *Psalm 7:1–2*

When David wrote this, Saul was out to kill him. He was to David a lion on the hunt, and David, as he had so many times before, realized that God was his only security in these or any circumstances. He knew the odds. Assassins were everywhere, and he was not expecting mercy from the psychotic, threatened king. David lived long enough to know that life wasn't fair, and this passage is devoid of self-pity. He has moved beyond the why-me? stage to the help-me stage. And God, in His own time, does answer David's prayer. It is Saul who is torn apart in the end and David who lives to old age.

We must be reminded that God is always stronger. We are not in a universe where a good lion and a bad lion are engaged in an eternal battle, where the tide swings this way and that and the outcome is uncertain. The great lion, the Lion of Judah (Rev. 5:5), King Jesus Himself, will prevail at the very moment He wishes to prevail—not a second too late or too soon, either. Satan is only allowed to exist to lose to the glory of God. Psalm 91 makes this clear:

> He who dwells in the shelter of the Most High,
>   who abides in the shadow of the Almighty,
> will say to the LORD, "My refuge and my
>   fortress;
>   my God, in whom I trust."
>
> *vv. 1–2 RSV*

David continues the majestic thought in verses 9–13:

Because you have made the LORD your refuge,
    the Most High your habitation,
no evil shall befall you,
    no scourge come near your tent.
For he will give his angels charge of you
    to guard you in all your ways.
On their hands they will bear you up,
    lest you dash your foot against a stone.
You will tread on the lion and the adder [a
        deadly viper],
    the young lion and the serpent you will
        trample under your foot.

You see, in 1 John 4:4 we are assured that "he who is in you is greater than he that is in the world." Jesus is in us—we who have trusted him—and Satan is in the world.

There's a great story that shows us how much greater God is than the circumstances that surround us. It is found in Daniel 6.

Daniel was a fantastic man by any measure and godly in the way I would like to be godly. Because of his gifts of leadership, wisdom, and efficiency, the king of Media-Persia, Darius, promoted Daniel to second in command of the entire empire. The other high government officials were angered by this and considered ways to remove Daniel from the king's favor. Their final plan was ingenious in many ways and, to some extent, it was the perfect crime. It would have worked, too, except for their failure to consider God's place in the equation. It just isn't prudent to forget about God while making plans. Their plan did, however, factor Darius into all their considerations. You see, he was proud and vain, and they knew they could count on him to be pompous. They also counted on Daniel's absolute devotion to God. To round out the plan, these conspirators took into account the irrevocable nature of the law of the Medes and the Persians and, ultimately, the savage nature of lions and their insatiable hunger.

Here's how they did it. They went to the king and suggested that everyone in the empire should pray only to Darius for thirty days. If a person defied the law and prayed to another god (or even the one true God), he or she would be thrown into the den of lions. This was one of the forms of execution used in this ancient empire—no one survived the lions. Darius humbly approved the new law, forgetting Daniel's absolute devotion to God. The king signed the edict, which, according to the law of the Medes and the Persians, was irrevocable. Once signed, this wicked edict became the law of the land and could not be changed or altered by anyone, not even the king.

Daniel prayed to God three times daily. And he was quite punctual in this habit. His political rivals documented that he had not prayed to Darius and formally charged him before the king with violating the new law. The king realized that he had been duped, but he could not change what had been decreed.

No one knows for sure how many lions were in the den into which Daniel was thrown (and Daniel was a man of some years by now), but the records from that time indicate that capital punishment and lion denning were not infrequent punishments. Some of these records indicate that a den may have had as many as forty ravenous lions in residence, all of whom enjoyed the exotic diet of royal castoffs. And Daniel was overweight (see Dan. 1:15), a real kosher McNugget.

Let's finish the story by reading the Scripture:

> Then the king commanded, and Daniel was brought and cast into the den of lions. The king said to Daniel, "May your God, whom you serve continually, deliver you!" And a stone was brought and laid upon the mouth of the den, and the king sealed it with his own signet and with the signet of his lords, that nothing might be changed concerning Daniel. Then the king went to his palace, and spent the night fasting; no diversions were brought to him, and sleep fled from him.
>
> Then at the break of day, the king arose and went in haste to the den of lions. When he came near to the den where Daniel was, he cried out in a tone of anguish and said to Daniel, "O Daniel, servant of the living God, has your God, whom you serve continually, been able to deliver you from the lions?" Then Daniel said to the king, "O king, live for ever! My God sent his angel and shut the lions' mouths, and they have not hurt me, because I was found blameless before him; and also before you, O king, I have done no wrong." Then the king was exceeding glad, and

commanded that Daniel be taken up out of the den. So Daniel was taken up out of the den, and no kind of hurt was found upon him, because he had trusted in his God. And the king commanded, and those men who had accused Daniel were brought and cast into the den of lions—they, their children, and their wives; and before they reached the bottom of the den the lions overpowered them and broke all their bones in pieces.

Then King Darius wrote to all the peoples, nations, and languages that dwell in all the earth: "Peace be multiplied to you. I make a decree, that in all my royal dominion men tremble and fear before the God of Daniel,

> for he is the living God,
> enduring for ever;
> his kingdom shall never be destroyed,
> and his dominion shall be to the end.
> He delivers and rescues,
> he works signs and wonders
> in heaven and on earth,
> he who has saved Daniel
> from the power of lions."

So this Daniel prospered during the reign of Darius and the reign of Cyrus the Persian.

Daniel 6:16–28 RSV

Lest you think Daniel got off without a thrill, remember that he was cast into the den of lions. In Daniel's day, animals were kept in pits, usually deep enough so they could not jump out. A lion's den would have been about fifteen feet deep. When Daniel was thrown into the den, no matter how you view it, that first step was a real doozie. Things continued to pick up when he realized that an angel was there to protect him. Perhaps the angel caught him, because the Scripture records that no kind of hurt was found upon him. And yet later in the story, the enemies of Daniel (and their families) were completely overpowered by the lions in the den—before they had even hit bottom. Every bone in their bodies was broken into pieces. Do you know how many people were thrown in that den after Daniel was pulled out? There were some 123 conspirators, their wives (many of the conspirators had more than one wife), and their children (these were older men, so they had many children, especially if they had more than one wife). I guesstimate the total number to be somewhere between seven hundred and a thousand. No wonder Daniel prospered! After he had been pulled from the den, he didn't have any enemies left in the kingdom nor anyone who would want to be an enemy. I think I like having God on my side.

Another familiar story in which a lion plays a prominent role is the story of Samson's wedding. The lion here poses two tests for Samson, one that he passes mightily and one that he blows in a big way. The following account concerns another servant of God who is protected from the tooth and claw of the king of beasts.

Then Samson went down with his father and mother to Timnah, and he came to the vineyards of Timnah. And behold, a young lion roared against him; and the Spirit of the LORD came mightily upon him, and he tore the lion asunder as one tears a kid; and he had nothing in his hand. But he did not tell his father and mother what he had done. Then he went down and talked with the woman; and she pleased Samson well. And after a while he returned to take her; and he turned aside to see the carcass of the lion, and behold, there was a swarm of bees in the body of the lion, and honey. He scraped it out into his hands, and went on, eating as he went; and he came to his father and his mother, and gave some to them, and they ate. But he did not tell them that he had taken the honey from the carcass of the lion.

Judges 14:5–9 RSV

Just for the record, the term "young lion," in this story refers not to a baby or a teenaged lion, but a lion in its prime. The writer of the Book of Judges wanted you to understand that Samson's strength was fully tested. A hand-to-paw battle with a lion, then, would be an optimum test of Samson's strength. He passed the first test, which was to trust God for incredible strength. He became strong only when the Spirit of God came upon him. Samson was able to tear apart the lion as one would tear apart a kid goat. (A baby goat's skin is thin and can be torn rather easily.) A lion's skin is thick and tough, and, of course, the lion has the strength of fourteen to twenty-one men. He aced the strength part of the test.

The second part of the test was a test of character and obedience. When Samson was young, he had taken a Nazarite vow. It was a vow that set him apart from other holy men. He was not only bound to keep all the rules that everyone was supposed to keep, but there were three more rules besides: (1) He promised not to have anything to do with any product derived from grapes, (2) he could not cut his hair, period, and (3) he could not touch a dead body, human or animal. If he did any of these things, he would have to start his life as a Nazarite all over, and that would begin by shaving his head and making sacrifices that would remove his uncleanness.

Now the Bible makes it clear that any animal that goes about on paws is an unclean animal and, of course, lions go about on paws (see Lev. 11:27). Samson ended up with a dead lion in his arms after the attack, and weeks later he went back and scooped honey out of the dead lion's carcass. Having done that, he should have gone through the ceremonial cleansing for having touched an unclean animal's carcass, but he did not want to lose his strength (not with the Philistines all around, watching for a moment of weakness on his part). Being obedient to God didn't fit into his plans at this time. Samson didn't grasp that it is our character, not our accomplishments, that are precious to God. He couldn't let go of being the world's strongest man, even during the period that it would take for his hair to grow out.

God was giving Samson an opportunity for spiritual maturity, but he remained a spiritual infant for his whole life. His was a life replete with self-indulgences and tantrums. All of his accomplishments were works of destruction. But God, by the power of His own Spirit, delivered Samson, and He will do that with or without scars for those of us who belong to Him.

The lion carcass was the first step down Samson's last road. Having found and shared the honey from this unique perch, Samson asked his father to contract a marriage for him to a Philistine woman. This didn't work out. Proud of his muscular exploits, particularly in overcoming the lion, he tried to impress some Philistines with his wit as well by proposing a riddle for them based on the lion and the honey. They compromised his wife (after all she was a Philistine first), and Samson found himself beholding to them, having lost the wager. Although the rest of the Samson story flows with the intrigue of tremendous action and adventure, Samson was never to find the true happiness that comes from following God and obeying Him. Yes, God was still able to use Samson for the good of His people, but in every instance that seemed to be in spite of this headstrong hulk.

Sometimes it's better to leave a roaring lion alone when you're not quite in God's good graces.

The figure of the lion in Scripture has many nuances. Looking over our shoulder, we see that it has been used as a warning to Christians to be on guard against the conspiracies of the devil (Samson could have used that particular warning). We know that we may have a few scars from the encounters along the way, but with God's help we'll have survived those confrontations with the roaring evil one, or, like Daniel, we'll have been protected from the claws of our hungry lions.

There's lions out there, but we travel with the greatest lion tamer of them all when we walk in faith with our Lord. When we do that, we see the lions at peace with all the animals they once preyed upon. And their roar will be heard no more.

2

BEARS

WHAT IS THE FIRST WORD THAT comes to mind when you think of bears? "Cute," "cuddly," "furry," a "teddy bear" perhaps? Or did you think of "grizzly," "ferocious," "dangerous"?

Naturally, your answers for this little word association game would depend largely upon your personal experiences with the animal.

One species of bear that many of us are most familiar with is the common, everyday, stuffed variety, called the Teddy Bear. They are most often found artistically displayed as part of a child's room decoration. Certainly the words "cute" and "cuddly" are appropriate descriptors for that setting.

"Dangerous," "ferocious." Now those are the words *I* recognize, along with a fraternity of experience-rich believers who work with bears and other animals on a daily basis. In fact, there is absolutely no doubt in my mind that people who work in zoos would rate bears as a zoo's most dangerous animal. I know I did. During the years I worked at a zoo, bears were the only animals to appear in my nightmares. Should you ever find yourself confronted by an angry bear, you would find no defense from its mighty strength and fury.

One particularly common species, and the one referred to in the Bible, is the Brown Bear. Today they are found on both the European and North American continents and throughout the Middle East. Grizzly Bears and Kodiak Island Bears are most likely a sub-species of the Brown Bear, but they grow to be several hundred pounds heavier than their European and Middle Eastern counterparts. The chief factor in this difference in size relates to the abundance and avail-ability of food in the various regions.

The Brown Bear of the Bible weighed in some-where between five to six hundred pounds, and at that weight would have the pulling power of at least twenty men. By comparison, the North American Kodiak Bear might weigh in at fifteen hundred pounds and have the pulling power of thirty men.

Many animals are capable of killing, but bears can make it a considerably gruesome event. For whatever reason, bears are likely to maul their victims time and time again, never really making it a point to put their prey out of their misery. They seem to be more inter-ested in immobilizing their catch rather than killing it. There have been cases where people have been attacked and mauled several times, but not killed or eaten.

Yellowstone National Park had a long history of safe Grizzly watching. That all ended one moonless night in the early 1960s when two Grizzly Bears, thirty miles apart from each other, attacked two separate campsites and pulled two girls, both eighteen years of age, out of their sleeping bags and killed them. In both cases, friends and boyfriends, who had climbed to the tenuous safety of the nearby trees, were helpless to ward off the vicious attackers. During the long night they waited, frozen with fear, aware that their young friends were already lost to them. When morning came, it was evident that the girls had been shaken like rag dolls by the powerful toothy jaws of the Grizzlies.

The story was published in the book *The Night of the Grizzlies*. There the author delivered a chilling account of animal mismanagement and the underestimation of one of God's most awesome creations, the Grizzly Bear—at the zoo where I worked, that text was considered powerful and popular reading.

About the same time as the Yellowstone catastrophe, our zoo also had a frightening bear incident. One of our Brown Bears, a particularly large one whom we called Barney, discovered that he could get his claws under the guillotine door that separated the bear compound into the display area and a holding area. Barney loved lifting that door—but he loved dropping it even more. A guillotine door slides up and down in a track. The top of the door is connected to a lifting device, but gravity holds it shut. This particular door weighed more than five hundred pounds, but Barney made it look like he was just sliding a window open.

At first Barney seemed to be satisfied to raise the door a foot and then let it drop. This made a terrible sound, and it became his way of telling the keepers that he wanted out. The noise was deafening and scared the other bears witless, at least until they got used to it. One day Barney took the exercise a little further.

Jeff, the bears' keeper that day, was working in the exhibit area. He dragged his high-pressure hose out and began his morning clean-up of the moat that ran through their enclosure. He looked back toward the door and was a little shaken to see that Barney was lifting the door higher than usual, causing it to bounce up and down on the concrete. Jeff made a mental note to tell his supervisor about Barney's advanced door dribbling and kept on with his cleaning chores. The water from the hose made such a loud noise that most of the time Jeff wouldn't have noticed the absence of the now familiar disturbance. But Barney's door game had been a part of his daily routine for so long that, when it stopped, the silence was deafening.

Jeff looked back to examine the silent door and his legs went a little limp. Amos, the largest of the two male Brown Bears, was entering the exhibit through the *open* door. Barney was letting him out!

As Jeff stood in the narrow corridor that was the passageway between the cages and the open area, he realized there was simply nowhere to go or to hide from the eight-hundred-pound giant lumbering toward him. He considered blasting the bear with the hose, but instantly dismissed the thought. He had no reason to think that Amos was angry, and he felt an urgent need to avoid antagonizing him. Everyone knows that angry bears are the worst kind.

Jeff opted to stand still and imitate the rocks and concrete around him. Fortunately, Amos ran past him without showing a spark of recognition. His only interest was obvious; he rounded the corner and dove into the pool for a morning swim.

But Amos had sideswiped Jeff pretty hard, allowing the keeper to feel the ripple of the awesome predator's shoulder and leg muscles. Jeff prayed, "Dear God, please don't let him smell me!" Not since childhood had Jeff remembered uttering a prayer of any kind, but he prayed very well for someone so out of practice. It seemed as though his prayer was answered, because Amos remained pleasantly occupied with his recreational bath.

Jeff turned to run to his access door; he had spent enough time "playing" with the bears. But that was not to be! Barney was still holding the door open, and now the two females, LuLu and Gertrude, were fighting each other to see who would be the next one through the opening. Their growling was a loud and low rumbling that Jeff felt with his whole body. He froze once again as he watched first one head then the other appear and disappear, each bear struggling to gain the first right of passage. No doubt about it, the first bear to clear the opening was really going to be irritated!

Finally, LuLu burst into the glory of the morning sun. She was so intent on joining Amos in the pool that she scooted through the corridor even more quickly.

Although Jeff was jostled about again, he was none the worse for wear.

Slowly, Jeff turned to see what Gertrude intended to do. She passed through the door slowly—and she was giving him a look of complete recognition. She paused, staring at Jeff with emotionless eyes. During what seemed like an endless ten seconds, she sniffed at him, her nose pressed against his trousers. She smelled the scent of the other bears, Amos and LuLu who had gone before her, but she also smelled the oppressive smells of a human. She snorted to clear the odors from her nostrils and then worked her overweight frame past Jeff and on to the pool.

Although he had arranged freedom for the others, Barney seemed unable to do so for himself. That was fortunate, indeed, for Barney was a mean bear and the most likely to taste Jeff. The door dropped. Its re-sounding crash startled Jeff, alerting him to the fact that this was his most convenient opportunity to leave the exhibit.

Realizing that he might not get a second chance, Jeff stumbled backward and threw himself through the access door. Pulling the hose through as fast as he could, he slammed the door and slid the hasp to the locked position. When he was sure that the door was secured he fell to his knees and lost his breakfast.

The humiliation that Jeff had experienced quickly turned to white-hot, full-blown anger, the kind of anger that generates irrational behavior. Had the zoo's architect been anywhere around that day, he would have found a bear keeper right in his face offering suggestions regarding less convenient access doors within the animal displays.

Jeff's reaction was based on his new firsthand knowledge of bears and their behavior. Three had decided to pass him by. Who knows why? They could just as easily have made sport of him for half of the morning, slowly tearing him to pieces as the Grizzlies in Yellowstone had done with their victims. Jeff knew what could happen. He was keenly aware that the most predictable thing about bears is that they are unpredictable, and that's what made him afraid.

The story of Barney and company and the Yellowstone tragedy should serve as reminders to us. We so often dwell on the gentle qualities of animals, we sometimes forget their destructive capabilities. The men and women of the Bible seemed to hold a deep respect for the latter. Many of the familiar stories make references to an animal's rage as if it were the "severe clause" of a well-deserved punishment. Often the reference is so brief it may have escaped notice, but the message is quite clear. Fear an animal's rage.

In the Bible, the first mention of bears is found in 1 Samuel, amidst one of the most loved tales of the Old Testament, the story of David and Goliath. David, the youngest of several brothers, was left at home to care for the sheep, while the brothers had been called to active service in the Army of Israel to battle the Philistines.

One day, David's father, Jesse, sent him to the battlefield with supplies for his brothers, but also to find out what was happening at the battlefront. When David arrived he discovered that Israel wasn't fighting at all, but for several days had endured the pompous challenges from a giant of a man named Goliath. He had offered a winner-take-all opportunity to anyone who would accept the challenge to fight only him. Goliath, who had been a soldier in the Philistine army since his youth, stood nine feet six inches tall. King Saul of Israel, the best soldier they had, was more than six feet tall, but he was afraid to fight the giant. The Army of Israel, humiliated, allowed the challenge to go unaccepted.

David found it difficult to believe that no one had taken a stand against the giant. After all, God would be on the side of the challenger. Although David was not more than fourteen or fifteen, he bravely volunteered. He was received into the court of King Saul to ask for the right to fight Goliath. This is where we pick up the Scripture:

But David said to Saul, "Your servant has been keeping his father's sheep. When a lion or a bear came and carried off a sheep from the flock, I went after it, struck it and rescued the sheep from its mouth. When it turned on me, I seized it by its hair, struck it and killed it. Your servant has killed both the lion and the bear; this uncircumcised Philistine will be like one of them, because he has defied the armies of the living God. The Lord who delivered me from the paw of the lion and the paw of the bear will deliver me from the hand of the Philistine."

Saul said to David, "Go, and the Lord be with you."

1 Samuel 17:34–37

The rest is history. David did the same to Goliath as he had done to the lions and bears who had threatened his flock. The description of his encounters indicated God's power in his life. If David literally grabbed a lion and a bear by the hair and killed them with his bare hands, it was by God's grace. It would take nothing less than a miracle to kill a lion or a bear in the way that David described—that and a "giant" step of faith.

Later, in 2 Samuel 17:8, David was a middle-aged, deposed king. His own son, Absalom, was leading a successful (but short-lived) rebellion against him. Absalom had two advisers, both of whom had served his father before him, named Ahithophel and Hushai. Ahithophel recommended that Absalom take twelve thousand of his men and kill David while he was weary and weak. Absalom approached Hushai for a second opinion:

Hushai replied to Absalom, "The advice Ahithophel has given is not good this time. You know your father and his men; they are fighters, and as fierce as a wild bear robbed of her cubs. Besides, your father is an experienced fighter; he will not spend the night with the troops. Even now, he is hidden in a cave or some other place. If he should attack your troops first, whoever hears about it will say, 'There has been a great slaughter among the troops who follow Absalom.' Then even the bravest soldier, whose heart is like the heart of a lion, will melt with fear, for all Israel knows that your father is a fighter and that those with him are brave."

2 Samuel 17:7–10

Hushai's description of David and his men fighting as fiercely as a she-bear robbed of her cubs is fearsome indeed. The maternal instincts of bears is legendary. I know firsthand how terrifying a mother bear can be. On a trip to Yosemite I managed to get myself between a she-bear and her cub and almost lost my life. (The whole story may be found in *Please Don't Feed the Bears*, pp. 19–29.) Their young are the priority of their lives; nothing alive would be safe from the wrath of a female bear if she thought her cubs were being endangered.

Let us also note, for the sake of motherhood, that female bears are capable of more than just the ferocious defense of their young. They are equally loving, playful, and attentive mothers also. They are good disciplinarians and patient teachers who would gladly die for their young. We mothers and fathers could take a few cues from their parenting skills.

Understandably, many of the teaching references concern the female bear's instinct to protect her offspring. She-bears exhibit intense and determined behaviors when the threat of danger exists. There's a

---

passage in 2 Kings, a magnificent story of the great and powerful prophet Elisha, but it is also an example of the fury of bears. Perhaps you recall this part of the story.

It seems that Elisha, who had performed many miracles and had given up great wealth to follow God's call, had a bit of a cross to bear. He was bald. In our society, that would not have been so terrible a burden. Baldness, as we understand today, is a result of a man's genetic heritage. In Elisha's day, baldness was looked upon as a weakness in character. And God had made Elisha bald. I'm unable to verify it, but that may have been one of the reasons that Elisha was so humble and so sensitive to the needs of his people. He was, however, a little touchy about his baldness, as you might detect from the following Scripture.

> From Jericho he went to Bethel. As he was walk-
> ing along the road, some young boys from the city
> began mocking and making fun of him because of his
> bald head. He turned around and cursed them in the
> name of the Lord; and two female bears came out of
> the woods and killed forty-two of them.
>
> *2 Kings 2:23–24* TLB

It is important to note that different translations of the Bible that render "youths" as "children" are leaving the wrong impression. The youths in this passage would be like a teenage gang. They would be like the Bloods, the Gypsies, and the Crypts who shoot people for fun, traffic in drugs, rape, and steal. They didn't frighten or bother Elisha, but they did remind him of an Old Testament passage that he decided was appropriate for the occasion, and I bet this was the last time any of the locals called anybody "baldy." I think Elisha remembered something from the Book of Leviticus:

> If you remain hostile toward me and refuse to listen to me, I will multiply your afflictions seven times over, as your sins deserve. I will send wild animals against you, and they will rob you of your children, destroy your cattle and make you so few in number that your roads will be deserted.
>
> *Leviticus 26:21*

This is the curse that Elisha called down upon the youths, and it was appropriate for those who showed hostility to God and/or the one whom God had sent. The scripture gives us a clear indication that we are to value what God brings to us and certainly not harass or ridicule his faithful servants. Those who make it their business to make life difficult for a pastor by insults and relentless bullying will someday face someone a great deal more frightening than two she-bears. That's not to say that pastors are unaccountable, but if they are innocent of wrongdoing and being harassed for not meeting the particular expectations of a selfish few—watch out! You will have God to deal with. Don't think for a minute He won't confront you for making life difficult for His servants. If they are trying their best and failing, encourage and help them, but leave them to God for removal. If your pastor's biggest sin is that he is boring—be careful. He may be good, kind, and loving to his sheep. If that's the case, then learn from his example, not his sermons. I've known other pastors who were well spoken but full of themselves. What I learned from them was that I didn't want to be like them.

Incidentally, the Middle Eastern Brown Bear, as described in the previous passage, would have had the pulling strength of about twenty men. Two bears against forty-two young men might even be considered a fair fight, but the bears destroyed them. Possibly, God meant to make the point: He and His servants are to be regarded with seriousness.

Some of the remaining "bear" passages are self-explanatory. Most of them describe the consequences we will face for making poor and self-serving decisions. Solomon uses the image of a face-to-face encounter with a bear to lay out a timeless admonition:

> Better to meet a bear robbed of her cubs
> than a fool in his folly.
>
> *Proverbs 17:12*

What kind of fools and follies do you think were in mind here? An addict or an alcoholic? A workaholic? Someone involved in a get-rich-quick scheme? What about a person willing to climb over anyone to get to the top? A thief? I wonder. In any case, the result remains constant—to run with fools is to jeopardize life and limb.

The prophets used the reputation of bears to paint a picture of the Lord's justice, and it is certainly a graphic argument for living within the bounds of the Lord's grace. Jeremiah and Hosea both refer to the ferocity of bears as a symbol of God's justice in allowing the fall of Israel and Judah and Jerusalem and the exile of His people:

> Like a bear lying in wait,
>   like a lion in hiding,
> [the Lord] dragged me from the path and
>   mangled me
>   and left me without help.
>
> *Lamentations 3:10–11*

> Like a bear robbed of her cubs,
>   [the Lord] will attack them and rip them
>   open.
>
> *Hosea 13:8a*

"Out of the frying pan and into the fire" is a common saying that applies to any instance when our bad choices worsen our situation. The Bible has an equivalent saying:

> It will be as though a man fled from a lion
>   only to meet a bear,
> as though he entered his house
>   and rested his hand on the wall
>   only to have a snake bite him.
>
> *Amos 5:19*

Anyone who has made a series of bad choices knows the feeling that comes with the frying-pan syndrome. But in context that is not all that this verse is trying to communicate. If you read Amos 5:20–6:14 you will see that God is telling people who are phonies that they cannot run away from His judgments. It is clear whether you look in the Old or New Testaments that God has a burning hatred of religious hypocrites, a hatred that burns white hot. He will not let us borrow or steal His glory. He desires authentic children and people who profess to love Him and tell others that they do. Those who serve themselves and their own interests make Him furious. In this verse we find a truth well worth remembering. If you decide to live as a phony, there will be no place you can be safe from the wrath of God.

I never tire of previews of coming attractions at movie theaters. And the prophet Isaiah gives us a preview of heaven with an unusual cast:

> The cow will feed with the bear,
>> their young will lie down together,
>> and the lion will eat straw like the ox.

Isaiah 11:7

The whole picture is one of the peaceable kingdom. And in Isaiah we find the redeemed world, which we will know when Christ returns, will be a world at peace and where the old natural instincts will be redeemed to the original instincts God had in mind at the time of Creation—a perfect world in perfect harmony with Him.

Perhaps there is one comparison that is as familiar today as it was to the writers of the Old Testament. Would this Scripture apply to anyone you know?

> We all growl like bears;
>   we moan mournfully like doves.
> We look for justice, but find none;
>   for deliverance, but it is far away.
>
> *Isaiah 59:11*

Although this passage says that our deliverance is far away and that justice cannot be found, it also acknowledges emotions and feelings common to us all. "We all growl like bears" is simply a way of saying we all get grouchy at one time or another. More than once my family has accused me of acting like a bear, and I must admit that I really do have that side to me, but I would like to be thought of instead as a *teddy* bear. I also "moan mournfully" from time to time, and I suppose that means I'm part of the world in which I live. Sometimes life isn't fair, and sometimes we are left in our trials for longer than seems reasonable. That's just the way life is in a fallen world, and we have to face it and live with it. We don't have to like it.

Acting like a bear occasionally is part of what it means to be human. But we also know that one day the bear in us will feed with the other animals in the perfect world to come.

3

SNAKES

IF IT IS TRUE THAT WE TEND TO HATE the things that we fear the most, then that explains in part why most people hate snakes. Why do we hate them so much? What inspires such fear?

In his fascinating work, *The Naked Ape*, Desmond Morris suggests that humans tend to fear animals that look the least human. We don't like snakes because they don't have arms and legs just as we don't like spiders because they have too many.

To further understand this human tendency to fear snakes, we should examine a few basic characteristics of snakes (or reptiles, or serpents) in general. The study of reptiles is called herpetology, whose name comes from the Greek word for serpent, *herpeton*, which means "creeping thing." Maybe you have already discerned why the term *creepy* has often been applied to snakes. It is fascinating, almost mystical, to watch a snake crawl. It seems to glide along as if propelled by magic. It is that unnatural movement, slithering along without the use of arms or legs, that is the basis for our suspicion of snakes.

Of course, there are other reasons why we fear these reptiles. One, in particular—some snakes are very poisonous. In the United States, statistics tell us that ten to twelve deaths occur annually from snake bites. That does not seem like many. Not quite half of those deaths are at the hands of a fanatical fundamentalist group which believes that handling poisonous snakes demonstrates a sincere faith in Christ's ability to protect them from the effects of the poison. That's a frightening thought, isn't it? It is even more frightening when we consider that they base this practice on a scriptural teaching:

> And these signs will accompany those who believe: in my name they will cast out demons; they will speak in new tongues; they will pick up serpents, and if they drink any deadly thing, it will not hurt them; they will lay their hands on the sick, and they will recover.
>
> *Mark 16:17–18 RSV*

I am not sure why these believers do not notice that there is no *command* or *imperative* in the passage, just the promise of protection should these things happen. Sadly, they feel that there is something to prove.

The remaining deaths are mostly children and people with high blood pressure who happen to step on or otherwise disturb a poisonous snake. In all, that number is quite low considering the total population that have encountered snakes at one time or another. Another reason for that low count is the estimate that U.S. rattlesnakes inflict "dry" bites as much as 60 percent of the time. This species has the ability to withhold venom, offering warning bites so as not to waste a lethal dose on something it surely could not eat.

Considering the "dry" bite factor, the fact that anti-venom drugs are readily available, and the fact that most people survive snake bites anyway, even if untreated, we see how foolish it would be to test that passage in Mark 16. Those odds don't equal a miracle.

In India the numbers of snake-related deaths are quite different. Ten to twenty thousand people die each year. These people have to walk wherever they go, most of them barefooted, and they are more susceptible to snakes. The species of snakes found in India are far more potent than those found in the United States, and there are far more of them. India has a nasty assortment of vipers, adders, and cobras that are very deadly. The Indian people also have less opportunity for medical treatment, so they face a greater peril than we will ever know.

Speaking of peril, remember when the Lord used fiery serpents to punish the Israelites in the wilderness after He had freed them from slavery in Egypt?

> From Mount Hor they set out by the way to the Red Sea, to go around the land of Edom; and the people became impatient on the way. And the people spoke against God and against Moses, "Why have you brought us up out of Egypt to die in the wilderness? For there is no food and no water, and we loathe this worthless food." Then the LORD sent fiery serpents

among the people, and they bit the people, so that many people of Israel died. And the people came to Moses, and said, "We have sinned, for we have spoken against the LORD and against you; pray to the LORD, that he take the serpents from us." So Moses prayed for the people. And the LORD said to Moses, "Make a fiery serpent, and set it on a pole; and every one who is bitten, when he sees it, shall live." So Moses made a bronze serpent, and set it on a pole; and if a serpent bit any man, he would look at the bronze serpent and live.

Numbers 21:4–9 RSV

We assume that the fiery serpents were vipers. The most common vipers in that area were sand vipers, usually called Saw-Scaled or Carpet vipers. They are abundant. There have been times in India when bounties were put on them in hopes of cutting down their populations. The symptoms of the viper's bite would be as follows:

1. Injection of venom initiates a fiery pain at the site of the bite.

2. Swelling begins right away and continues in relation to the amount of venom injected and the individual's tolerance of venom.

3. Discoloration at the site of the bite varying from white to flaming reds, purples, and dark blues.

4. Victims experience nausea and vomiting,

accompanied by excruciating stomach pains and cramping.

5. Victims usually experience extreme thirst.

6. Diarrhea is not uncommon.

7. The liver and kidneys are damaged from filtering toxins, resulting in extreme tenderness in the lower abdominal area.

8. Hemorrhaging occurs in the form of nose bleeds or bleeding from the mouth or eyes.

The viper's venom is hemotoxic, destroying blood cells and causing bleeding where capillaries are close to the surface. A person may bleed to death internally and experience a gradual weakening until life slips away. Quick deaths from a viper's bite would be very unusual. Generally, the suffering would prolong for one or two days.

In Bible times, there was no treatment for snake bites, so chances of survival were very slim. You can understand why the people were anxious to repent of their complaining. They were given more than enough incentive to get their act together.

That incident in the wilderness is brought into focus in a spectacular way when, in the Gospel of John, Jesus says:

And as Moses lifted up the serpent in the wilderness, so must the Son of man be lifted up, that whoever believes in him may have eternal life.

John 3:14–15 RSV

What Jesus means is that all of us have been bitten by a deadly viper and we are dying. Just as the children of Israel had to look at the serpent that Moses made so that they might be saved, we must look to Christ, trusting Him for our salvation.

The venom that threatens our lives was planted by a deadly serpent a long time ago in the Garden of Eden. That venom is called sin. Jesus will gladly supply the antidote if we will admit we have the disease and ask Him for help. I sometimes wish that the symptoms of sin were as dramatic as the bite of the fiery serpents in the wilderness. Those kinds of symptoms would surely bring us to repentance as they did the children of Israel. And God wills that we seek Him because of our great need for Him and our love for Him. But the choice is ours to make—"For God so loved the world that he gave his only Son, that whoever believes in him should not perish but have eternal life" (John 3:16 RSV).

That is the cure. Jesus is the antidote for our sin. Sin is the venom in our lives, and we are dying because of it. All of us need the cure. We can't get along without it. There is plenty for everyone, and it's only available from one source. He is glad to be able to offer it to all who would come asking.

The slithering serpent's literary image covers both ends of the spectrum. You know, of course, that the serpent is most often used to symbolize aspects of evil—poison, pain, death, deceit, trickery, cowardice, the enemy, and the devil. But did you know it is also used to symbolize good things—wisdom, wonder, miracles, and cures. We find snakes in the handful of fortunate animals that are sometimes symbols for Christ. The bronze serpent that Moses cast and held up to save his people was a symbol of Christ. It had the power to save and heal.

The serpent also has the distinction of being one of the animals that Jesus said we should be *like*.

> Behold, I send you out as sheep in the midst of wolves; so be wise as serpents and innocent as doves.
>
> *Matthew 10:16* RSV

That was one of the Scriptures that gave me fits during my zoo years. The phrase "wise as serpents" troubled me. For one thing, snakes are not extremely intelligent animals. Although they can be conditioned, they will never learn anything that could improve the quality of their lives. They are born knowing every single thing they will ever need to know. They have the kind of knowledge commonly called instinct. It is knowledge that is a genetic hand-me-down, shared with each subsequent generation. Snakes just emerge from the egg knowing how to hunt, hide, and hibernate like professionals. So, if all of that is instinct, why did Jesus say, "wise as serpents"? It doesn't make sense.

I studied this riddle often and without success. Then my patience and persistence were rewarded. I worked out my problem by asking the question,

What makes a snake a snake? I believe that Jesus singled out the snake because of a characteristic that He considered wise. The answer had been staring me in the face for months. Jews considered watchfulness one of the main characteristics of wisdom. To be watchful is to be on guard, aware, careful. If you watch what you're doing, you make fewer mistakes. If you keep watch, you are ready for your enemy. If you are watchful, you live longer and better. These things show wisdom.

Now when God made the animals, He made the snake more watchful than any other. During the whole of its life, it never closes its eyes. It cannot, because God designed it without eyelids. A snake keeps watch 24 hours a day, every day, 365 days a year. Can you imagine never closing your eyes? We have to blink in order to lubricate our eyes, but a snake's eyes are lubricated by another means. They are protected by a clear scale which is located directly over the eye. This scale is actually a part of the snake's skin and is shed and replaced by a new eye scale or eye cap each time it sheds its old skin. There is a clear liquid between the scale and the eye so that the eye is always lubricated.

How watchful is a snake? I'm glad you asked. The snake sleeps, but the eyes continue to see objects that might affect its survival. For instance, if a snake were napping on a rock and a leaf fell from a nearby tree within the snake's field of vision, the snake would remain asleep. If the snake were to see the shape of a hawk, a coyote, or an eagle, it would awaken and crawl to safety. That's the ultimate in watchfulness. It's sort of like David's approach when he said, "I have hidden your word in my heart that I might not sin against you" (Ps. 119:11).

Remembering the context of the verse you can see that this is just what Jesus meant to convey. He was sending His disciples out like sheep among wolves, so it would be absolutely imperative to be watchful. Our very survival would depend upon it. Do you remember 1 Peter 5:8? "Be sober, be watchful. Your adversary the devil prowls around like a roaring lion, seeking some one to devour" (RSV). Yes, snakes give us our best look at the wisdom of being watchful. Jesus wants us to be like them, snakes, that is! Isn't He full of surprises?

Snakes really are amazing once you get beyond the fear of them and discover that they are one of God's very best creations. They have some very admirable qualities.

1. You've heard the saying "Cleanliness is next to godliness"? Well guess what? The snake is the cleanest and most disease-free animal on Earth. At the base of each scale is a tiny oil gland that secretes and coats the scale in front of it. When the oil dries, it becomes so smooth and hard that nothing sticks to it. Snakes crawl through mud, dust, and carnage and stay slicker than STP. They don't spend any time cleaning or grooming themselves. Occasionally, after eating, a snake may rub its face on a rock to make sure that nothing unsightly or inappropriate could be hanging from its mouth.

2. Snakes are not only observant, but they are extremely sensitive; they are "feeling" oriented. The viper has a labial pit on each side of its face, inside of which is a heat-sensitive nerve. There are many times when a viper crawls through grass and cannot see its prey. Not to worry. The snake can feel better than it can see. The viper turns its head from side to side until each heat-sensitive nerve detects the same temperature. It can sense a quarter-degree of temperature difference five feet away. If it strikes at a heat source when its nerves are experiencing the same temperature, it will hit the source with deadly accuracy.

Missile guidance systems were designed after the heat-sensing capability of the viper. They were first used to guide our so-called Sidewinder missiles.

3. A snake has a terrific mechanism for finding food. As it crawls, it licks the air with its delicate forked tongue. The tongue has a sticky substance that attracts molecules in the air. When the snake withdraws its tongue and rubs it across a sensing organ in its mouth, it is able to distinguish specific molecules. If sufficient numbers exist, the viper will curl up and wait for the chance to snatch its prey.

4. Snakes have incredible patience and endurance. My family owns a gopher snake whom we named Samson. He has lived with the family for eight years. He is four feet long, very gentle, nonpoisonous, and has been handled by thousands of children over these eight years. I have taken him to classrooms,

camps, and churches as a teaching example of God's amazing handiwork in nature.

About five years ago, Samson escaped from his aquarium. We tore the house apart looking for him. After much time had passed, we began to think he was forever lost to us. I thought he had somehow found a way out of the house and crawled away. Still, everyone in the family kept an eye out for him. As the weeks turned into months, we all accepted the reality that this gentle, lumbering, old bull snake was probably out of our lives for good.

At the time, we were renting a house and the time came when we needed to move so that I would be closer to work. I was driving thirty-four miles each way, every day, over crowded California freeways. We packed everything and loaded it onto a large truck. It was getting dark when the last load was packed. We went back into the house to rest for a minute, get something to drink, and check again for anything we may have forgotten.

When finally we got up to leave, I noticed that my keys were missing. That wasn't odd. I am absent-minded, and they are always missing. I was not worried, just inconvenienced and a little annoyed for choosing this particular time to be just like myself. We looked in several places for the keys and didn't find them. Thinking that the keys may have fallen out of my pocket while I was laying on the landlord's couch (the only thing we were leaving behind), I returned to the couch and began removing cushions.

It was a hide-a-bed. I pulled the bed out, exposing the mattress and something else that came as a great surprise. A snake skin was woven in and out of the hide-a-bed's springs. It was Samson's shed. Carol and I then turned the couch upside down and there, high in the back of the couch also woven in and out of the springs, was Samson looking at us from his dark private hiding place.

It had been nearly six months since we had seen our family pet. I carefully removed him from the springs and held him under a light to see how he was doing, having gone without food and water for six months. To tell you the truth, I could not see any real difference in his appearance or weight, although he did take an awfully long time to quench his thirst that evening.

I have often wondered what would have happened if we had left without recovering Samson. Most people wouldn't have shared the joy we felt when we found the old fellow. "Those that wait upon the Lord will renew their strength." Six months? Snakes are the personification of patience, endurance, and restraint.

5. Snakes are at their best after they have been in the light for a while. When I first read the passage in Proverbs, I wondered what Agur was seeing in the way of amazing behavior when he saw a serpent sunning on a rock. They are cold blooded by nature but adapt to the surrounding temperature. The colder they are, the slower they move and the less likely they are to catch food. They warm up when they are in the

light, and that's when they are at their best. When snakes are warmed by the light, they do what they do best—hunt. Snakes were created to hunt.

We do what we do best when we have been walking in the light, rather than walking in darkness. We were made to love and serve God. We will make the right moves and will be more responsive to God when we walk in the light as He is in the light.

The other side of the coin reflects the dark images that we receive from the serpents. Did you know that they figure into Solomon's description of what being an alcoholic is all about? He said:

> Who has woe? Who has sorrow?
> Who has strife? Who has complaining?
> Who has wounds without cause?
> Who has redness of eyes?
> Those who tarry long over wine,
> those who go to try mixed wine.
> Do not look at wine when it is red,
> when it sparkles in the cup
> and goes down smoothly.
> At the last it bites like a serpent,
> and stings like an adder.
> Your eyes will see strange things,
> and your mind utter perverse things.
> You will be like one who lies down in the
> midst of the sea,
> like one who lies on the top of the mast.
> "They struck me," you will say, "but I was
> not hurt;

they beat me, but I did not feel it.
When shall I awake?
I will seek another drink."

Proverbs 23:29–35 RSV

How is the serpent used in this passage? It's used
to describe the turning point in the life of an alcoholic.
The wine goes down smoothly at first, but once inside
it begins to do bad things. It causes hallucinations, and
the alcoholic is like a man who is drowning or tossed
around at sea, out of control. He loses feeling and self-
control. He isn't *taking* a drink, the drink is *taking* him.

I have seen that in my own family because wine
was my mother's drug of choice. She became everything that this verse describes before she finally
drowned in the wine she looked to for relief. It eventually relieved her of her life. She took an overdose of
prescription drugs and thus ended her own life.

That verse is very personal to me. I am not a fan of
alcohol. I know, as only an abandoned son can, what it
can do to a mother if it gets the chance. That stuff can
put you through a slow death just as surely as if you
had been bitten by a viper for an adder. I watched my
mother die that death for years.

In the passage in Proverbs 23, we see the serpent,
or wine, as representing two concepts: deception and
betrayal. Wine looks beautiful, desirable, and deli-
cious, but then it slowly destroys. It promises joy but
delivers depression, strife, and chaos and takes control
of you.

Another detail from the dark side of a serpent's nature is that it diligently pursues the task of punishing the wicked. The following verses show how God uses the serpent as a curse or judgment against them.

> He [the wicked] will suck the poison of asps;
>   the tongue of a viper will kill him.
>
> *Job 20:16 RSV*

It was not until much later that men understood that the tongue of a serpent was soft and absolutely harmless. The hollow fangs, usually located at the front of the mouth, do the dangerous business.

With Israel's pursuit of wickedness, God became quite irritated and issued this frightening judgment:

> And I will heap evils upon them;
>   I will spend my arrows upon them;
> they shall be wasted with hunger,
>   and devoured with burning heat
>   and poison pestilence;
> and I will send the teeth of beasts against
>   them,
>   with venom of crawling things of the dust.
>
> *Deuteronomy 32:23–24 RSV*

> Their wine is the poison of serpents,
>   and the cruel venom of asps.
>
> *Deuteronomy 32:33 RSV*

"For behold, I am sending among you serpents,
adders which cannot be charmed,
and they shall bite you,"
says the LORD.

Jeremiah 8:17 RSV

Needless to say, these verses indicate that when God has had enough nonsense from His people, He doesn't mess around. After reading this, who would put Him to the test? I hope you don't make the mistake of thinking God has changed. Some would have us believe that God had changed His perspective by New Testament times. If that were the case, then the Apostle Paul would never have cautioned us with these words from his first letter to the Corinthians:

We must not indulge in immorality as some of them did, and twenty-three thousand fell in a single day. We must not put the Lord to the test, as some of them did and were destroyed by serpents; nor grumble, as some of them did and were destroyed by the Destroyer. Now these things happened to them as a warning, but they were written down for our instruction, upon whom the end of the age has come.

1 Corinthians 10:8–11 RSV

But the good news is that the righteous have nothing to fear from serpents. The following incident from the life of Paul is found in Acts 28. Paul was being taken back to Rome as a prisoner. The ship ran aground and more than two hundred passengers had to swim ashore. Miraculously, all of them survived the shipwreck. Luke tells us:

> After we had escaped [death], we then learned that the island was called Malta. And the natives showed us unusual kindness, for they had kindled a fire and welcomed us all, because it had begun to rain and be cold. Paul had gathered a bundle of sticks and put them on the fire, when a viper came out because of the heat and fastened on his hand. When the natives saw the creature hanging from his hand, they said to one another, "No doubt this man is a murderer. Though he has escaped from the sea, justice has not allowed him to live." He, however, shook off the creature into the fire and suffered no harm. They waited, expecting him to swell up or suddenly fall down dead; but when they had waited a long time and saw no misfortune come to him, they changed their minds and said that he was a god.
>
> *Acts 28:1–6 RSV*

This is what Jesus had in mind when He said these signs would follow those that believe; "They will pick up serpents." Herein the prophesy is fulfilled. God demonstrates that He can and will take care of His own. Did you notice that Paul endures despite unfair circumstances? There is no complaining on his part. He is unfairly imprisoned. He is shipwrecked in a strange land. It's rainy and cold. A viper has the gall to bite him after he has been gathering firewood so everyone else can be warm. Then the people accuse him of terrible crimes he has never committed. Paul just waits it out continuing to do wonderful things for everyone else under circumstances most of us would hate to have to endure. The reward is evident. Paul had joy, one of the fruits of the Spirit. He loved his ministry. The Book of Acts closes with Paul under house arrest in Rome. Yet we still get the feeling he's happy.

> And he [Paul] lived there two whole years at his own expense, and welcomed all who came to him, preaching the kingdom of God and teaching about the Lord Jesus Christ quite openly and unhindered.
>
> *Acts 28:30–31* RSV

The day will come when no one will ever have to fear snakes again. We have this wonderful picture of our future in the Book of Isaiah:

> The wolf shall dwell with the lamb,
>   and the leopard will lay down with the kid,
> and the calf and the lion and the fatling to-
>   gether,
>   and a little child shall lead them.
> The cow and the bear shall feed;
>   their young shall lie down together;
>   and the lion shall eat straw like the ox.
> The suckling child shall play over the hole of
>   the asp [cobra],
>   and the weaned child shall put his hand on
>   the adder's den.

> They shall not hurt or destroy
>   in all my holy mountain;
> for the earth shall be full of the knowledge of
>   the Lord
>   as the waters cover the sea.
>
> *Isaiah 11:6–9 RSV*

This passage is a preview of the coming of Heaven. No more fear, for the earth will be full of the knowledge of the Lord.

This chapter is about snakes, but I want to conclude it by offering a revolutionary thought. It's the kind of thought that you might immediately reject at first because you have always thought about something in a particular way. I want to suggest that when Satan appeared to Eve in the Garden of Eden he was not in the form of a large snake, but instead he appeared as a red dragon. Consider this passage from the Book of Revelation:

> Then I saw an angel coming down from heaven, holding in his hand the key of the bottomless pit and a great chain. And he seized the dragon, that ancient serpent, who is the Devil and Satan, and bound him for a thousand years, and threw him into the pit, and shut it and sealed it over him, that he should deceive the nations no more, till the thousand years were ended. After that he must be loosed for a little while.
>
> *Revelation 20:1–3 RSV*

All the information we need is in the second sentence of the passage—"the dragon, that ancient serpent, who is the Devil and Satan." The two words that Scripture uses to designate *serpent* are *herpeton* and *ophis*. These words are similar to our word *reptile*, which covers a whole spectrum of animals, including snakes, lizards, frogs, turtles, alligators, and crocodiles—essentially any cold-blooded animal with scales. The Greek word *drakon* (dragon) would be a clarifying word to let us know what kind of *herpeton* or *ophis* was being talked about. We do not know what kind of serpent God was naming in Genesis 3 until we get to Revelation 20.

Satan has been known to take more than one form. As an angel, he would have looked similar to a man with wings. When he possessed Judas Iscariot, he certainly appeared as a man, but for reasons perhaps only known to God and to the devil himself, he chose to exist in the form of a dragon. We have bits and pieces of Scripture so that we are able to describe him.

In Revelation 12, Satan is described as a great red dragon with seven heads and ten horns and with seven diadems on his heads. Diadems are kingly ornaments used to adorn turbans and tiaras. This dragon has a tail so powerful that it knocks one-third of the angels out of heaven and casts them down to earth. The biblical text says that his tail swept a third of the stars from heaven, and I believe that the host of angels in heaven is here referred to as the stars of heaven.

The reference to the seven heads is probably a symbolic statement to let us know that this dragon is very intelligent. The ten horns are either indications of weaponry or, as in rams' horns, instruments of praise. The diadems reflect the stature of the dragon. He was, or thought he was, royalty. In the Bible, the numbers seven, ten, and twelve are used to denote completion or perfection. By any standard this is an awesome creature. The Revelation 12 passage describes the dragon's nature as murderous in the worst way. It says that he intended to kill the baby Jesus as soon as He was born. No human saw him in Bethlehem that day, but Satan was present at the birth of Christ.

Revelation 12:7–9 sets forth more of the great dragon's history:

> Now a war arose in heaven, Michael and his angels fighting against the dragon; and the dragon and his angels fought, but they were defeated and there was no longer any place for them in heaven. And the great dragon was thrown down, that ancient serpent, who is called the Devil and Satan, the deceiver of the whole world—he was thrown down to the earth, and his angels were thrown down with him.
>
> *Revelation 12:7–9* RSV

The dragon was pretty impressive until he confronted the Lord's angels. Then he fell and lost everything. Ezekiel wrote someting about the fall of evil in his twenty-eighth chapter. The prophecy is directed to the king of Tyre, but we know by the things that are said that the king is hopelessly possessed of Satan himself. Read the following and see what you think. Note that the italicized lines could only be true of Satan.

Moreover the word of the LORD came to me: "Son of man, raise a lamentation over the king of Tyre, and say to him, Thus says the Lord GOD:

"You were the signet of perfection,
full of wisdom
and perfect in beauty.
You were in Eden, the garden of God;
every precious stone was your covering,
carnelian, topaz, and jasper,
chysolite, beryl, and onyx,
sapphire, carbuncle, and emerald;
and wrought in gold were your settings
and your engravings.
On the day that you were created
they were prepared.
With an anointed guardian cherub I placed you;
you were on the holy mountain of God;
in the midst of the stones of fire you walked.
You were blameless in your ways
from the day you were created,
till iniquity was found in you.
In the abundance of your trade
you were filled with violence, and you
sinned;
so I cast you as a profane thing from the mountain
of God.

Ezekiel 28:11–16 RSV

76

The six verses above are the chronicle of a perfect being becoming evil. Five things are said in these verses that could not be said of anyone except Adam before the Fall and Jesus when he was on earth.

1. The being is addressed as "the signet of perfection" and described as "perfect in beauty." That was how Satan began his existence. Not one of us could ever have been described as perfect. We are all flawed.

2. "You were in Eden, the garden of God." We know that only five beings were in the Garden of Eden: the Lord, Adam, Eve, the serpent, and an angel with a flaming sword who kept anyone else from being an accidental tourist. The Tree of Life was replanted in Heaven, and the garden was either destroyed before or during the flood of Noah's time.

3. "On the day that you were created" would not have been said to any human except Adam. Angels were created, not born. So we can assume God is addressing an angel, which again allows us to see that the serpent was a fallen angel. Jesus always existed.

4. "You were [past tense] blameless in your ways." Meaning that the fallen angel/dragon/serpent used to be sinless. That could only be said of Adam, Eve, or a fallen angel. Jesus remained sinless.

5. "I cast you as a profane thing from the mountain of God" could only have been addressed to a fallen angel. No human has ever been in heaven on the mountain of God. Jesus is there, and Satan goes there daily to accuse the saints.

These five things could only be true of the great dragon mentioned in Revelation. And this is why I believe that the serpent in the garden was a dragon.

The dragon's prime characteristic is also found in the Genesis story:

> Now the serpent was more subtle than any other wild creature that the LORD God had made.
>
> *Genesis 3:1 RSV*

Subtlety is a very scary term. The word used in Genesis 3:1 is translated as *crafty* in 1 Samuel 13:3. In Exodus 1:10, it is rendered as *shrewd.* In the New Testament it's translated in Acts 7:19 as *craftily,* and in Acts 13:10 as *villain.* Matthew 26:4 translates it as *stealth,* and 2 Corinthians 11:3 uses it to mean *cunning.*

All of these terms are words used to describe predators—animals that kill and eat their prey. We would describe a fox as crafty, because foxes execute elaborate plans to avoid their own predators and catch their prey. Shrewd is, of course, the way shrews act. A shrew has long been considered—ounce for ounce—the most tenacious, focused, bloodthirsty killing machine known to man. They will attack animals several times their own size, and stay on them until they have killed the animal. Stealth is the way of the tiger and the leopard as they quietly hunt their prey and grab them when they are most un-aware. Cunning describes coyotes and wolves who work together with their group, carefully following plans that lead to the death of their prey.

The great dragon, the ancient serpent, the deceiver, the Devil, Satan is nothing less than the most awesome predator of all time. Jesus said of him, "He was a murderer from the beginning. . . . When he lies, he speaks according to his own nature, for he is a liar and the father of lies" (John 8:44 RSV). He is focused, as a serpent unblinkingly focuses on its prey, and his powers of destruction are beyond imagination. The tragedy is that he gets us to do most of his dirty work for him. He uses what has proven time and time again to be a pretty effective tool—temptation. My father taught me that temptations were promises that didn't work out the way we thought they would. Satan offers what God has forbidden, and we buy it, but Satan never gives us what we thought we were getting. Buying anything from Satan is like deliberately shooting your foot, except shooting your foot would be smarter than believing anything the devil is offering us.

Satan never did anything in anyone's interest but his own. His chief desire is to kill us, and he will use any and all methods at his disposal to accomplish this end. Suicide is his favorite tool. He offered it to Judas Iscariot, and Judas took him up on it, even though Jesus would have forgiven him for his betrayal. Satan would gladly convince us that we have committed a sin that Christ's love is not sufficient to forgive. That is not so. Pride leads us to believe that our sin is greater than God's love. That thought is a lie direct from the pit. Don't believe it! There is always hope, and there is always God's grace.

How powerful is Satan? When he is captured and thrown into the great pit, an astounding question is asked concerning him:

> Is this the man who made the earth tremble,
>   who shook kingdoms,
> who made the world like a desert
>   and overthrew its cities?
>
> *Isaiah 14:16–17 RSV*

Don't sell this dragon short. He's one tough cookie! And his bite is worse than his bark. Count on it.

4

CAMELS

Almost anyone who has seen a camel believes the old saw that it looks like a horse designed by a committee. Only when you compare one camel with another are you apt to say that one is a handsome specimen. They are not beautiful in form, nor are they colorful. There is not much in their temperament to commend them to us as pets. Yet I find them to be one of the most interesting, outstanding, and astounding animals created by God. They are the epitome of not being able to judge a book by its cover.

Camels brought Abraham out of Ur of the Chaldees, provided an excuse for a messenger to begin the marriage brokering of Rebekah and Isaac, ate with the flocks of Job, provided the beginnings of David's wealth, brought the people of the Exile back to the land of their fathers, and provided a punch line for two of Jesus' sayings. You might say that camels are all-purpose biblical animals. Surely there weren't many animals in the Middle East that were larger than camels.

There are two fine passages concerning camels that we will look at later, but the greatest lessons involving camels are learned by studying the animal itself. Almost everything about them is admirable, but they do have two undesirable qualities: bad tempers and questionable loyalties.

Most dictionaries don't have a definition for "beast of burden," they just have pictures of camels. The name "camel" comes from the ancient Hebrew word *Gamel*, which translates as "carries a burden." This of course was what they were domesticated to do, and no animal does it better. Camels can carry loads equal to their own weight for short distances. The average weight of a working camel would be about twelve hundred pounds, but it can weigh as much as twenty-two hundred pounds.

The camel is the biblical equivalent of the eighteen wheeler, the original "Saudi Semi." For more than four thousand years they have been the principle means of transporting goods through the desert. Caravans were made up of camels, sometimes hundreds of camels, carrying precious cargo across waterless wastelands along the edge of the desert. The ancient Middle East could never have prospered as it did without camels.

Burden carrying, however, even under the best of conditions, is the pits. And like it or not, bearing loads is and has been the camel's destiny.

Few of us would choose to be burden bearers if we were not under orders, but then we are ordered to share one another's burdens. Galatians 6:2 says so, plain as day, with no way around it: "Bear one another's burdens and so fulfill the law of Christ." That means getting involved with things we would much rather not do. In Galatians 6 it means helping someone who has been sinning to be restored. It means comforting those who are burdened with pain. It means helping the sick, the imprisoned, and the aged.

There are burdens all around us. They are not hard to identify. There is someone you know whose child is on drugs, whose husband or wife is leaving them. There is someone in your circle of friends who lost a struggle with temptation or was just diagnosed with cancer. The burdened are all around us. They are as common as air. Each of us must take inventory and answer the question "Are we hiding from or helping the burdened?"

When the Bible says "bear one another's burdens," it assumes that we all have them, and having them is not an excuse for our not reaching out to someone else who has them. We need to be like camels. We, by the Lord's command, must be burden bearers; we must be the Lord's camels.

Camels are uniquely equipped to survive in the desert. The desert is among the harshest environments on the earth. As we discovered during the Persian Gulf War, temperatures in the desert can range from 30° in the early morning to 110° in the afternoon. Months can pass without rain, and then it can rain with such fury that the ground cannot absorb the water fast enough to avoid flash floods. It rains less than seven inches a year in the desert, which of course is what makes it a desert. The survival of all life in the desert is tied to water; no water leads eventually to no life.

Desert winds blow with enough force to knock a person down, and the blowing sand is blasted into your eyes, your face, or any exposed part of your body. The sting of the sand is like the sting of hornets.

Though the desert is very harsh indeed, the camel is up to the task of surviving in it. For example, God complemented the eyes of the camel with long, pretty, functional eyelashes. These lashes serve as a screen to protect the camel's eyes from blowing sand. In addition, the camel has a third eyelid that can be raised and lowered like a storm window. The membrane that makes up this third eyelid is clear, and the camel can see through it. Though those around them loose their way, camels are equipped to find their way when things are not clear.

We seem to lose our way rather easily. It doesn't take much for us to be blinded or to make us close our eyes to the harsh realities surrounding us. But it is then that we discover that we too have been given a wonderful tool to use in finding our way. That tool is faith, and it is the ability to see through life's dense fog, driving rain, and blowing sand to see the better times ahead. Faith helps us to keep our focus.

King Jehoshaphat was in a mess, and it seemed obvious to him that he and his people were on the verge of annihilation. But he decided to look at his situation through the filter of faith, and prayed to God: "We do not know what to do, but our eyes are upon thee" (2 Chron. 20:12 RSV). And the Lord delivered Judah.

Sometimes we need to pray to the Lord the way the great King David did, saying:

> Open my eyes, that I may behold
> wondrous things out of thy law.
>
> *Psalm 119:18* RSV

Only the Lord can keep us focused. He has given us his promise to be with us through thick and thin if we only have faith—faith to be able to see and understand that things are under control when that's not what seems to be the case. Paul said, "For now we see in a mirror dimly, but then face to face." Things aren't always clear to us, but they are to God. He is our seeing eye. His Word teaches that we are to walk by faith, not by sight, because what we see is often an illusion, especially if what we see seems to indicate that our side is losing.

When the disciples saw Jesus arrested, they thought they were watching the end, but we know that what they were seeing was just the beginning. Like camels, we often need to filter what we see so that we do not lose our way. Camels use their eyelashes and special membrane to see what's ahead; we use faith and trust in God. How well are you seeing now? Do you need to say, "I do not know what to do, but my eyes are on thee"?

We've all had someone turn and say to us, "If you can't stand the heat, get out of the kitchen." That's a good saying for those of us who can get out of the kitchen, but there are times when we just can't. Many of us are like the witch in Hansel and Gretel, stuck in the oven with the door shut.

Camels live in an environment that makes it impossible to get out of the sun and sunglasses are out of the question. God has given camels a body that creates much of its own shade and a head bone that grows out over the eyes to protect them from the relentless blinding light in the all-but-shadeless desert.

We are weak and most of us cannot survive violent extremes. When we feel as if we are in a blast furnace of hardship, when the heat of demands is wilting us, we have a shelter in the Lord. The Scripture calls this shelter The Shadow of the Almighty. David left these comforting pictures of this shelter in the Psalms:

> He who dwells in the shelter of the Most High,
>   who abides in the shadow of the Almighty,
> will say to the Lord, "My refuge and my
>   fortress;
>   my God, in whom I trust."
>
> *Psalm 91:1–2 RSV*

> The Lord is your keeper;
>   the Lord is your shade
>   on your right hand.
> The sun shall not smite you by day,
>   nor the moon by night.
>
> *Psalm 121:5–6 RSV*

CAMELS

We need to learn to live in the shade of the Almighty. Like the camel, we already have the necessary tools to endure the heat, but unlike the camel, we must choose to use them.

Desert heat creates another problem: the frequent need for water in a place where water is scarce. Camels are terrific when it comes to solving the water problem. God designed them so that they can store a large amount of water in their muscle tissue. A thirsty camel can drink up to fifty gallons of water at one sitting, which would be more than four hundred pounds of water. Food energy, not usable water, is stored in the camel's hump, which is primarily made up of fatty tissue. On a desert journey a person would collapse if he lost 12 percent of his body's fluids. A donkey would drop if it lost 25 percent of its fluids. But a camel can lose more than 40 percent of its liquid and keep on going.

There are cases on record of fully loaded camels marched for eight days without water in the extremely arid area of Somalia. More impressively, a group of camels were led on a thirty-four-day journey without water, and they covered 537 miles. However, only a few of these animals were able to recover from this Herculean feat; most of them had been taken past the point at which an animal can recover. These animals died tragically, having given everything and more than they had to give to their masters whom they trusted too much. This march occurred in Australia, which has more than fifty thousand working camels.

My point in mentioning the camel's phenomenal ability to persevere is that we Christians need some of the grit that makes a camel do that. Self-denial doesn't seem to be our cup of tea. "Make do with what you have" does not seem to be the battle cry of our generation. Instead, we prefer to inscribe our samplers with a motto like "I want more, and I want it now!" But endurance and self-sacrifice are wonderful characteristics and presently in short supply amongst our species.

Jesus said, "He that endureth to the end shall be saved" (Matt. 10:22 KJV). And the Bible says, "As you know, we considered blessed those who have persevered. You have heard of Job's perseverance and have seen what the Lord finally brought about. The Lord is full of compassion and mercy" (James 5:11); and "But if you suffer for doing good and you endure it, this is commendable before God. To this you were called, because Christ suffered for you, leaving you an example, that you should follow in His steps" (1 Pet. 2:19–20).

It is clear from a sampling of the Scripture like this that the quality of endurance is a prized character trait. God would have it in all of us. Not only God, but teachers, trainers, coaches, employers, generals, and friends would love to see this quality in us because with it we can be counted on. Without it we can't. This is the trait that lets us finish what we start. It's a camel-like quality and perhaps it's the camel's best quality.

Another trait of camels is their desire to stay pure, so to speak. When a camel is thirsty and comes upon a dirty or polluted watering hole, it moves on, waiting for the water that is pure. In a sense it waits for God's best. Camels have a discerning ability to go along with their qualities of endurance and perseverance. When a sandstorm rages, a camel uses its muscles to close its nostrils and block out the sand. It breathes through its mouth, and the hairs around the mouth act as a filter so that the camel's lungs remain clean. The animal simply excels at remaining clean on the inside. It doesn't allow anything into its body that would do it damage.

Camel hair is also amazing. Somehow it keeps them warm in the winter and cool in the summer. How does it do that? I'm sure there is a scientific explanation, but I don't know it and am quite satisfied just to acknowledge that this is the way God made the camel.

One could go on and on about camels. We use their hair to make expensive sport coats and overcoats. In the Middle East their milk is prized and their meat is considered a delicacy. They can run as fast as race-horses, and the more of them you own the wealthier you are perceived to be. That has always been the case in the Middle East. But camels do have two bad traits worth mentioning, for we possess them also.

Camels have very bad tempers, and they tend to hold grudges. If riled, they can stomp a person flatter than a frisbee.

The Los Angeles Zoo had a Bactrian Camel (the two-humped species) named Ali that had frequent mood swings, only his moods swung from grouchy to enraged. He was never what you would call a happy camel. If he ever was in a good mood he hid it from those of us who cared for him. He may have been a closet smiler, but it was a very small closet. Grouchy animals bring out the worst in grouchy animal keepers. Through the years I saw several keepers who found a perverse joy in ensuring that an animal like Ali had a good reason to be in a bad humor.

Harry, one of our senior keepers, was such a person. He would entice Ali to the fence with a handful of succulent (think like a camel here) alfalfa hay. Then, when Ali stuck out his tongue or lips to take it, Harry would take a pair of pliers, grab the camel's lips, and hold Ali in place. He would snarl things like, "You think you're really something, don't you Ali? Well, you're not so tough, now are you? You just remember who you're messing with, you stinking piece of desert snot." It kinda makes you wonder who gave Harry the camel duty.

Ali remembered Harry real well. And he waited patiently for his chance to show Harry how he felt about him.

One day Harry went into Ali's exhibit to do some light clean-up, and he forgot to be watchful of Ali. Harry was in his sixties, but Ali was in his prime. Ali saw Harry, and he felt a long-standing, righteous anger begin to well up from deep within his being. That smoldering anger then exploded into a volcano of vengeance. The camel charged Harry, and the hapless keeper turned to run. The effort was futile though, because Harry was no match for the athletic, agile, eighteen-hundred-pound "stinking piece of desert snot" focused on his destruction.

Ali ran into him. Harry felt as if he'd been hit by a car. He was in shock. Before he could comprehend what was happening, Ali sank his sharp canines into Harry's right leg and clamped down on it like a vise. Ali lifted Harry off the ground, and Harry began to scream for help. He was dazed, but he had been around animals long enough to know when one was trying to kill him. People said they could hear Harry's screams half a mile away. Ali lifted him high into the air and dashed him to the ground. Harry screamed louder than ever. Ali dashed him against the ground again, and Harry was almost a goner. He could feel muscles tearing, and he was fighting unconsciousness. He knew that if he fainted, Ali would stomp on him until there was no sign of movement, no life.

Ali tried to place a hoof on Harry's chest to crush him, but Harry was tough for an old man and fought to roll aside. Out of the corner of his eye he saw Raul entering the exhibit with a scoop shovel, and the sight of help gave him the strength to resist a moment longer.

Raul thought that Harry was getting some of what he deserved, but he couldn't let Ali kill him, because the Zoo might have to destroy Ali, and that wouldn't be fair. Raul swung his shovel as hard as he could, hitting Ali in the head. But Ali was so focused on

killing Harry that he showed no reaction to the formidable blast. Raul hit Ali again, and he apparently felt it
this time because he dropped Harry and backed away.
Raul never took his eyes off of Ali, but he reached
down and grabbed Harry's arm and began dragging
him out of the exhibit. Ali, still angry, followed, hoping
for another crack at Harry but settling for regurgitat-
ing some stomach acid all over him.

I know of no other incident at the zoo where a
man came closer to meeting his Maker. Harry was
hospitalized and suffered severe backaches for the rest
of his life. I know Harry, and I don't believe he had
made any preparations to meet his Maker, so I was
glad he lived a while longer. I was also glad to hear
that he retired from animal care, for he was
undeserving of the honor of caring for God's handiwork. I also heard that Ali has been doing better since
then, with a kinder keeper and more than enough
alfalfa straw to keep the average camel happy.

In my opinion, the second character flaw of camels is worse than their having a temper. (It may not be
worse for some, but it really fries me.) Camels will
usually be kind to their handlers as long as they must
depend on them for their food and water. When food
and water abound, camels don't need anyone anymore. They have no sense of loyalty or friendship,
even when they have received nothing but tender
loving care from everyone (except for a few Harry's of
course). If the water is flowing, if the grass is green,
then it's "Forget you, see you later, au revoir, don't call

me, I'll call you." Fair-weather friends are nobody's idea of ideal companionship.

There are two "camel" verses in the New Testament that express great wisdom and truth. The first is Matthew 23:24, and it's simple and to the point: "You blind guides! You strain out a gnat but swallow a camel."

Jesus said this to a group of people whose priorities were way out of line. They had traded their love for God and people for a new love: they loved to be admired for keeping rules. They usually did the right things, but they did them for all the wrong reasons. Their motives were upside down. Their hearts were dark and self-centered. They wanted the praise that others would normally give to God.

Jesus' illustration was actually very funny and not unlike the humor of some of our contemporary comedians. Steve Martin once sang, "It's just impossible . . . to get a Cadillac up your nose . . . it's just impossible!" To one in Jesus' audience, swallowing a camel would be just as impossible and just as funny. I bet this line got a big laugh, but not from the people about whom Jesus was speaking. Jesus is painting a picture of someone picking a tiny gnat out of some soup and then turning right around and *accidentally* swallowing a camel. He is saying that we notice the unimportant things and let the most important things escape from us. He is accusing them of majoring in the minors and being petty. Worst of all, these people were causing everybody else to become more concerned with loving rules than loving each other. That kept people so busy with the rules that they had little energy left to love God and to love those around them. They were changing everyone's focus to being out of focus.

When everything becomes important, nothing becomes important. The attitude of these Pharisees (that's the brand name of legalistic rule-keepers Jesus was talking to) took all the fun out of life and made big deals out of things God never meant to be big deals. Well, Jesus nailed these guys, and you may want to reread the whole speech in Matthew 23 just to refresh your memory.

We evangelical Christians can be just like the Pharisees: pretty petty when we want to be. If we are not careful we may find ourselves sifting gnats and swallowing camels. We try to establish our own goodness and spirituality by comparing our behavior with the behaviors of other people, both believers and nonbelievers. We have been awfully hard on smokers and drinkers, although the Scripture has made it crystal clear that "there is nothing which enters a man that can make him evil. It is what proceeds from the heart of a man that makes him evil." Gossip is running unchecked in our churches, prejudice is alive and well, and greed has sunk some deep roots. But let someone light a cigarette just outside the sanctuary, and our immediate assumption is "There's a person who needs God." I met a lady recently who confessed that she found herself doubting anybody's faith in Christ if she or he hadn't heard of James Dobson.

We need to get back to cherishing the things that Jesus cherished. Jesus cherished loving the Lord our God and our neighbor as ourselves. He cherished humility, self-sacrifice, and truth. Jesus loved it when people's deepest needs were met and hurting people were comforted. He liked seeing the poor cared for and children taught to love and trust God. Jesus emphasized things like faith and hope and good attitudes. He loved it when people repented when they didn't get it right. He thought it was terrific when people tried their best to help others to entrust their lives to Him. And Jesus loved a cheerful giver.

Frankly I don't think He is overly concerned about smoking, musical preference, hair styles, earrings, and clothing. If we sweat the small stuff, we don't have time to be concerned with the things of great value to God. Camels remind us to keep focused on what's really important.

Jesus thought of the camel again in Luke 18:25 (the same story is also told in Matthew 19:24 and Mark 10:25): "Indeed, it is easier for a camel to go through the eye of a needle than for a rich man to enter the kingdom of heaven" (Luke 18:25).

We all know this story. Most people take one of two ways in approaching this passage. Some have tried to make a case for a very small gate in the wall of Jerusalem, called The Needle's Eye. Supposedly, this was the smugglers' gate and getting camels through it was quite a task. The camel had to be unloaded, in-cluding its goods and its saddle. The wares were carried through the gate and then the camel was forced to its knees and made to crawl its way through. This procedure was time consuming, inconvenient, and definitely not a natural movement for camels. Crawling is not one of their special gifts, and they resist it with enthusiasm. This routine was not impos-sible, but The Needle's Eye was one of the most diffi-cult ways to get into the city.

The other approach brought to the passage is that Jesus was setting up an impossible situation. This second view holds that Jesus was literally referring to a sewing needle. Of course it would be impossible for a camel to pass through the eye of a needle. So what Jesus was saying was that the rich couldn't get into heaven—period.

Now when we look at the life of Christ we know that some believers and followers of the Lord were rich: Lazarus, the brother of Mary and Martha, was rich and a believer. Nicodemus the leading teacher of Israel was rich and a believer. Joseph of Arimathea was rich and a believer. We know this because it was his expensive tomb, hewn out of solid rock, that Christ was given for burial. This would seem to indicate that it is not impossible for the rich to get into heaven, just difficult. Not many would make it. Like the camel in the first view, they would have to give up their load and crawl through the entrance on their knees. And most rich people find it very difficult to give up their possessions and crawl. It wouldn't come easy, but it wouldn't be impossible either.

We do get some help by placing the verse in the context of the story from which it comes. It all began when a rich young yuppie came to Jesus and asked him the most important question that anyone can ask: "What do I have to do to be sure that I'm going to heaven?" Jesus more or less said, "You know as well as I do: you have to keep the commandments." The yuppie told Jesus that he had been keeping the commandments since his childhood. He must have felt empty inside, because as yet Jesus hadn't told him anything he didn't know, and he still wasn't sure heaven was where he was headed. Jesus waited a moment and said, "One thing you still lack. Sell all that you have and distribute it to the poor, and you will have treasure in heaven; and come and follow me." This was a major disappointment to the young man because he was very rich. Jesus looked at him, and you could tell he was very sad. Finally He said, "How hard it is for those who have riches to enter the kingdom of God! For it is easier for a camel to go through the eye of a needle than for a yuppie to enter the kingdom of God." Those who heard Jesus teaching the story were obviously amazed and had to ask, "Then who can be saved?" They knew quite well a camel (probably the largest animal they could imagine) couldn't go through the eye of a needle (probably the smallest opening they could imagine).

When we ourselves realize that God is our first priority, that our relationship with Him is the most important thing in our lives, we find that camels and needles don't necessarily have to go together. Although Jesus said that it was easier for a camel to go through the eye of a needle, he didn't say that a camel *had* to go through the needle's eye in order for a rich person (that is, someone whose wealth supposedly indicated a blessing from or favor with God) to enter into heaven—he said, in effect, it was impossible. The effect of his statement is easily measured by the distress of his audience—"Who then can be saved?"

Camel or no camel, needle or no needle, Jesus said, "What is impossible with men is possible with God." And God has been slipping camels through the eye of the same needle for a few millennia.

As interesting as the first approach to understanding this passage is, we lack substantial proof that a gate called The Needle's Eye actually existed. Looking back at the question that Jesus was answering, we know that no one has the resources to buy an admission ticket to heaven. Who could put a price on the love of God in Christ Jesus? No one can get there without God's help. We are at His mercy. Thank goodness for His grace! He must be at the forefront of our lives—preceding our own lives, our families, and our accumulated possessions. Without God's help, heaven would be out of our reach forever.

Whereas Jerusalem's old wall may never have known an opening called The Needle's Eye, the entrance to the road to heaven is a needle's eye. By the grace of God brought to us through His Son, we navigate that tiny opening with an act of faith and trust. Our long trek is not yet over, we have a ways to go to get to the heavenly gates. But just beyond that threshold is a fountain of living water to quench the thirst of all the Lord's camels.

5

OXEN

W HEN WAS THE LAST TIME you saw an ox? The chances
are very good that it was probably a *picture* of one
pulling a covered wagon across the prairie. Most of us
would not know an ox if we saw one. Actually, the
term *ox*, or *oxen*, is a general reference that comes from
the term *bullocks*, meaning bull. *Bous* and *tauros* are the
Greek words for ox. Usually an ox is a castrated bull,
and therefore a more or less misfortunate bovine. It is
difficult to distinguish just which animal may be
indicated in a passage of Scripture because ox or cattle
translate from the same word.

Somewhere in their history, wild oxen interbred
with cattle and the result was a very strong animal. In
this way, oxen lost their vicious, unpredictable nature
and could be trained to do strenuous work. They were
used to haul wagonloads of commercial goods and to
plow the fields; the latter increased agricultural efficiency beyond most farmers' wildest dreams. Oxen
were the original tractors, if you will. Together with
horses and donkeys, oxen were the mainstay of any
farming enterprise, serving as an indispensable partner
in agriculture advancement. Remarkably, they have

remained that way for more than four thousand years.

In Third World countries today, teams of oxen still pull plows and draw cartloads of goods to market. Oxen have proven to be fuel efficient and ecologically sound farming implements, giving back to the environment that which they take away.

The Bible speaks of oxen many times and often describes the oxen as being yoked. A yoke of oxen means two. The yoke was the wooden frame placed over the shoulders of two oxen, attached with strong leather tack, and connected to a cart, plow, or wheat-milling device. This was one of the original applications of the abstract idea of harnessing power and bending it to a preferred use. In the ancient near east, only the well-to-do could afford a yoke of oxen. It followed naturally that the more you owned the wealthier you were (some ideas have been around for a long time). Given the extraordinary power of oxen versus donkeys and their being particularly suited for plowing and hauling, owning a large number of oxen was indeed a status symbol.

Oxen were quite large in size. A bull ox might weigh close to two thousand pounds, a full ton of power, and be capable of enduring many hours of work. When oxen weren't working, they might lazily graze for eight hours and then rest for up to sixteen hours afterward.

What might we learn from oxen? Genesis 49 is the first mention of oxen in the Bible. Jacob, the patriarch of the twelve tribes of Israel, was dying. He gathered all of his sons to him so that he might give them his last words. Some might see this as a reading of the will. In this case, it was a dying father's last chance to commend his praiseworthy children and chide the sluggards.

Jacob said wonderful things about Joseph, his eleventh son, who really was one of the greatest men who ever lived. And he praised Judah, who was in the lineage of Christ. But three brothers received a serious dressing down.

Reuben, Jacob's firstborn son, took a good tongue lashing for a terribly immoral act. By law and custom, he should have inherited the largest share of his father's estate, but against the merits his father saw in him, he received nothing because he had slept with one of his father's wives. This would be a great wickedness now, but in those days it was even more so. Jacob, although he may have forgiven Reuben, made him pay dearly for that wicked night.

Jacob's second and third sons, Simeon and Levi, however, received even worse. Because of their cruelty, Jacob was clearly ashamed to be their father. He said:

> Simeon and Levi are brothers;
>> weapons of violence are their swords,
> O my soul, come not into their council;
>> O my spirit, be not joined to their company;
> for in their anger they slay men,
>> and in their wantonness they hamstring oxen.

Genesis 49:5–6 RSV

Simeon and Levi were the only brothers to have no land for their descendants. You must know how important land was to the children of Israel. It's what they lived and died to protect. Simeon was given a little share of Judah's land, but it was soon absorbed by Judah's descendants. Levi received nothing. Why?

Two reasons were given. They were murderous and cruel both to men and animals. "In their wantonness," Jacob says, meaning that they didn't play by any rules, they chose to ignore the laws of decency, which was apparent from the fact that they had a habit of hamstringing oxen. That means that they slit the muscles and tendons of the animal's back legs so that it could never walk again. If the animal wasn't put out of its misery, it would lie there for several days slowly dying. For some reason, Simeon and Levi found a perverse pleasure in this. Animal cruelty must have been considered a great evil to have been mentioned as one of the two reasons that Jacob's sons were disinherited.

Jacob was understandably upset by the mistreatment of animals because he was a shepherd. It is no surprise that his pronouncement of punishment against Simeon and Levi was severe.

This is a powerful message: God loves animals. They are an important segment of Creation. After all, the Lord created animals before He created humans. They were considered good, just as everything was at the time of Creation. Of course, they weren't sufficient in and of themselves to complete Creation—that was reserved for God's last act of Creation, namely, humans. But they are a part of His universe, and as such, He cares for them.

The proverbs say, "Blessed is the man that hath regard for his animals." You can't be happy if you're cruel to animals, and you can't be happy outside the approval of your father. Jacob didn't put up with animal cruelty, and God won't either. Succinctly stated, the moral of that story of Simeon and Levi is that all of us should be kind to animals.

From another part of the Old Testament, in the discussion of the Ten Commandments, there is a direct and indirect mention of oxen. In the fourth commandment we are told that after six days of work we are to observe a day of rest and make the Lord the primary focus of our life:

> Six days you shall labor and do all your work, but the seventh day is a Sabbath to the LORD your God. On it you shall not do any work, neither you, nor your son or daughter, nor your manservant or maidservant, nor your animals, nor the alien within your gates.
>
> *Exodus 20:8*

In this commandment we notice the be-kind-to-animals concept again. We are reminded that even those who are as strong as an ox also need rest. In this day and time, children have parents who are driven by the demands of the workplace and, as a result, are unable to experience any rest. Driven people produce driven children, destined for high anxiety and a shorter lifespan. These parents will be able to provide everything their children need except for time spent together and the closeness that keeps love fresh in a family.

If animals require rest from their labors, then so should people. An ox may be used all week to pull the plow required to plant the crop. It may be used all week to pull the machinery needed to harvest the crop. But no animals had to work the every-day-at-my-desk schedule that today's driven workers face. If animals can't keep up that kind of pace and survive, we can't either. The livestock always had time off because they needed to replenish their strength for the tasks ahead. No farmer would endanger his livestock by working them to death. He utilized them wisely. These were expensive animals. This was a significant investment. He paced them through the work necessary to make the farm functional and efficient and profitable. The Lord knew what He was doing when He mandated a day of rest for everyone.

Oxen are also mentioned in the tenth commandment, which deals mainly with personal happiness.

> You shall not covet your neighbor's house. You shall not covet your neighbor's wife, or his manservant or his maidservant, or his ox or donkey, or anything that belongs to your neighbor.
>
> *Exodus 20:17* NRSV

Oxen were the Mercedes Benz of farming implements and they were highly prized, but they were not to be coveted. Coveting makes it impossible to feel satisfied or fulfilled, impossible to be thankful for what we do have. Coveting robs us of our ability to want what God wants for us. It is a prideful sin, because it assumes that we may raise our own stature by reducing that of our neighbors. The trouble is, there is so much to want, that wanting more only seems to increase our appetites. What a tiresome business!

From the lofty description as the Mercedes of farming, we see an altogether different perception of oxen in Exodus 21. Oxen have been known to demonstrate a rather cantankerous nature on occasion. Actually, we could go so far as to say it is a violent nature:

> When an ox gores a man or a woman to death, the ox shall be stoned, and its flesh shall not be eaten; but the owner of the ox shall be clear. But if the ox has been accustomed to gore in the past, and its owner has been warned but has not kept it in, and it kills a man or a woman, the ox shall be stoned and its owner also shall be put to death.
>
> *Exodus 21:28–29* RSV

You may not have realized that there were occasions where capital punishment was appropriate for animals. In this case the ox is not being held morally accountable for its actions since it has no understanding of right and wrong. Rather, it is destroyed to prevent it from killing again. And that responsibility rests with the owner, who would suffer a similar fate if the problem is not addressed.

The Bible places the highest value on human life and holds each of us responsible and accountable to preserve it. Not only is the ox used as an example of the value of human life, it also underscores our need to be responsible to protect each other and respect each other's property rights.

> When a man leaves a pit open, or when a man digs a pit and does not cover it, and an ox or an ass falls into it, the owner of the pit shall make it good; he shall give money to its owner, and the dead beast shall be his.
>
> *Exodus 21:33 RSV*

We have a saying for this: "You break it—You bought it." The point the Scripture makes is that we are always responsible for our own actions and the actions of our pets or animals. There is a prevailing attitude these days that says, "Plead innocent, no matter what, and get off as easily as you can." If we take a long view of justice, we must realize that God will mete out justice in the end anyway. There are folks with brilliant lawyers who manage to escape punishment for their crimes. But God is fair, and one day we will all get what we deserve. Shouldn't we then be asking the question: "Am I responsible?" rather than "How do I get out of this?" Everything in Exodus

21:33–22:16 covers this issue completely. In a nutshell it says:

1. Take responsibility for your own actions.
2. Make fair contracts that make it clear who is responsible when something bad happens.
3. Be reasonable.

These things are really not too much to ask, are they? And how they help us get along later!

The following is my favorite ox passage. It's a zinger!

> You shall not see your brother's ox or his sheep go astray, and withhold your help from them; you shall take them back to your brother. And if he is not near you, or if you do not know him, you shall bring it home to your house, and it shall be with you until your brother seeks it; then you shall restore it to him. And so you shall do with his ass; so you shall do with his garment; so you shall do with any lost thing of your brother's, which he loses and you find; you may not withhold your help. You shall not see your brother's ass or his ox fallen down by the way, and withhold your help from them; you shall help them to lift them up again.
>
> *Deuteronomy 22:1–4* RSV

This passage is called the good neighbor policy. If you see someone who's really hurting, you may not pass them by. Help them. If ever there was a call to get involved, it is found in this passage. It is almost impossible to read this and not know that God expects us to be doing something to make His world a better place. (Incidentally, I must add that this passage also leaves no doubt that God is calling us to help hurting animals as well as hurting people.)

Ask yourself: "What am I doing to further the cause of Christ?" So many of us have grown sleepy and lukewarm. Do you want to do something? Call your pastor; he will put you to work.

Another meaty concept is found in Deuteronomy:

> You shall not plow with an ox and an ass together.
>
> *Deuteronomy 22:10* RSV

Why not? Because the ox will end up carrying the load. Animals are just like people, they always take the path of least resistance. It wouldn't be ten minutes and the donkey would discover that if it just walked along the ox would do all the work. The ox outweighs the donkey by some sixteen hundred pounds. They are unequally yoked.

A marriage involving a Christian and one who is not is also an unequal yoke. If the purpose of life is to glorify God, Christians will find that their purpose is not equally pursued and will soon feel as if they are pulling the full weight of the marriage alone. Christians feel called to join other Christians in worshiping God, but the non-Christian spouse will feel abandoned, and there will be a struggle. The two will be pulled apart as they pull in different directions. Often believers just give up and live with the guilt of a weaker faith rather than continue to struggle with their spouses. Today, Christians joined by marriage are struggling to stay together as never before, but the death rate of unequally yoked marriages is astounding. Although it doesn't seem so bad at first, eventually the strain of inequality becomes evident, and the bridge of communication collapses.

During the last six years, I have served as pastor to the single parents at the First Evangelical Free Church of Fullerton. I have been a part of more than six thousand counseling sessions and thirteen thousand phone calls dealing with floundering marriages. I wish I could convey the heartbreak that comes out of unequally yoked marriages. I know many under my care who would have me tell you not to do it. It is a nightmare. It doesn't work out. Such a marriage is akin to an ox's being yoked with an ass; their mutual work is never completed.

A further look at oxen takes in the passage in 1 Kings where we find a story of the great prophet Elijah. God has just told him that it is time to take an early retirement and that he will be replaced by a younger man of faith named Elisha. On our first occasion to meet him, the Scripture tells us that Elisha is plowing with not one, not two, but twelve yoke of oxen. His family must have been loaded! At the same time, Elisha must have been a super Arnold

Schwarzenegger to tire out so many teams of oxen
during the course of a day's plowing. Here's how the
Scripture tells us about the first meeting between
Elijah and Elisha:

> So [Elijah] departed from there, and found Elisha
> the son of Shaphat, who was plowing, with twelve
> yoke of oxen before him, and he was with the twelfth.
> Elijah passed by him and cast his mantle upon him.
> And he left the oxen, and ran after Elijah, and said,
> "Let me kiss my father and my mother, and then I will
> follow you." And he said to him, "Go back again; for
> what have I done to you?" And he returned from
> following him, and took the yoke of oxen, and slew
> them, and boiled their flesh with the yokes of the
> oxen, and gave it to the people, and they ate. Then he
> arose and went after Elijah, and ministered to him.
>
> *1 Kings 19:19–21 RSV*

Elisha is one of many who demonstrated their
willingness to give up their old life and follow after
God. But nobody ever did it more willingly than
Elisha. The young rich man couldn't do it after Jesus
told him give his money and all that he had to the
poor so that he might follow Him. But Elisha is different. He sees the wonder of serving God as the highest
of callings. He immediately says good-bye to his
beloved mother and father, slaughters his oxen, all
twenty-four of them, cooks them, and then feeds the
people. Talk about willingness to burn your bridges
and sacrifice for God. This was a doosie of an example.

This was a prime sacrifice done in the blink of an eye. He had his values together.

A modern-day Elisha, Nate Saint, could identify with this way of thinking. He was willing to risk his own death so that the Auca Indians might know God's gift of eternal life through Jesus Christ. Nate said, "It is a foolish man who is not willing to give what he cannot keep to gain what he cannot loose." There isn't one of us who wouldn't benefit from pondering what our faith has cost us. If it hasn't cost us anything, that is probably what it is worth. Following Jesus always means leaving something of value behind. Try to name a great saint who didn't.

Whether our things of value are given up or taken away, the point is that God will unfailingly provide for our needs. Whatever things of great value have been set aside for the sake of our Lord are probably not all that necessary in the first place.

Now Job was a man accustomed to sacrifice and hardship. He had everything of value taken from him. He had been a wealthy man, owning, among other things, over a thousand oxen. Satan stripped him of all his wealth, including his oxen. He was left in absolute poverty with no way to get his wealth back. After a time, the Lord restored Job to more wealth than he had ever known before. He was given two thousand oxen and double everything else that he had lost, except his children. The Lord gave him the same number as before, because the first ten were in heaven waiting to be reunited with their earthly father.

We should remember that whenever God takes something of great value from us, He intends to replace it with something of greater value. We honor God with our willingness to lay down our valuables before Him, then trusting that He will take care of our every need.

Through it all, the oxen pull. Their name denotes strength and size. Their basic qualities are dependability and perseverance. For these reasons they were highly valued in the agricultural world of the ancient near east. To any farmer, his oxen were like money in the bank. The crop would be planted and the harvest would be brought in, because his oxen always answered the call to work.

6

PIGS

D<small>O YOU LIKE PIGS? I DO</small>, and I know I'm not the only one. Think of all the pigs who have achieved star status: Porky Pig, Mr. Zuckerman's famous pig Wilbur (from *Charlotte's Web*), Arnold from "Green Acres," Jim Henson's famous Miss Piggy, and of course the Three Little Pigs. More recently, we've met *Misery*, the pet pig from Stephen King's novel by the same name. Even our Los Angeles County Fair uses a Porky-like Pig as its mascot and logo.

Pigs are very intelligent animals, nearly as intelligent as dogs and cats. If it weren't for their size and the mess they make, they'd make nice pets.

The Bible has many things to say about pigs, but in only one instance can one of these passages be considered complimentary, and it's an indirect statement at that. The way I read it, on the day of Creation when God made the animals, He said they were good. I suppose that includes pigs. As we delve further into the Scriptures, we find that pigs are used most often as bad examples. The books of Leviticus and Deuteronomy get right down to the business of telling us that pigs are undesirable animals.

The pig is also unclean; although it has a split hoof, it does not chew the cud. You are not to eat their meat or touch their carcasses.

Deuteronomy 14:8

And consider, as Isaiah does, the destiny of people who eat pig's meat:

Of those who eat the flesh of pigs and rats and other abominable things—they will meet their end together, declares the LORD.

Isaiah 66:17

It would seem that the Lord takes a rather dim view of His people eating pork. Why would that be? Well the answer is easy. The Lord cares about the health of His people. Perhaps of all the animals that humans have eaten, the pig is the most disease ridden. Being totally omnivorous, they eat anything within their reach that appears to be edible. They eat roots and tubers that they dig from the ground with their snouts and tusks. They eat all manner of vegetables and fruits. They eat rodents, mice, and rats. They eat birds. They also eat snakes, both poisonous and nonpoisonous. They eat *anything*. They eat things that have died of diseases which humans can contract.

The most notable disease that humans can catch from pigs is trichinosis. Trichinosis is a disease that pigs contract when they eat a food contaminated with tapeworms. The tapeworms migrate through the intestinal wall of the pig until they come to lie dormant in its muscles. A ham is a muscle and is located at the upper portion of the pig's hind leg. These tapeworms are very tough to kill and can survive a good deal of heat. If the ham we eat hasn't been cooked sufficiently, we will ingest the tapeworm and its deadly cycle will continue with us. We might also contract swine fever—a potentially fatal virus. Because of its indiscriminate eating habits, any disease that the pig has ingested could be passed into our systems. Does this add a new dimension to the expression, "You eat like a pig"? It is literally the pig's lack of good taste that has earned it the distinction of being the king of the unclean and lacking in the ability to discriminate.

Listen to what Jesus says in the Book of Matthew:

> Do not throw your pearls to pigs. If you do, they may trample them under their feet, and then turn and tear you to pieces.
>
> *Matthew 7:6*

You see, pigs have no values. They don't know pearls from marbles. Not knowing the difference, they have no capacity for appreciation. Having no discernment, they ingest everything and become polluted, or as the biblical language phrases it, unclean. They want everything and value nothing. They are the world's most convincing example of filth and waste.

But as bad as pigs are, there is one story that demonstrates to me that they are not without limits. They do have some limited sense of discernment. Luke tells us this story of the swine drawing a line:

> They sailed to the region of the Gerasenes, which is across the lake from Galilee. When Jesus stepped ashore, he was met by a demon-possessed man from the town. For a long time this man had not worn clothes or lived in a house, but had lived in the tombs. When he saw Jesus, he cried out and fell at his feet, shouting at the top of his voice, "What do you want with me, Jesus, Son of the Most High God? I beg you, don't torture me!" For Jesus had commanded the evil spirit to come out of the man. Many times it had seized him, and though he was chained hand and foot and kept under guard, he had broken his chains and had been driven by the demon into solitary places.
>
> Jesus asked him, "What is your name?"
>
> "Legion," he replied, because many demons had gone into him. And they begged him repeatedly not to order them to go into the Abyss.
>
> A large herd of pigs was feeding there on the hillside. The demons begged Jesus to let them go into them, and he gave them permission. When the demons came out of the man, they went into the pigs, and the herd rushed down the steep bank into the lake and was drowned.
>
> *Luke 8:26–33*

See! There is something pigs won't tolerate. They may eat rats and dead things which still carry tapeworms and disease. They may eat snakes and nose around in the dirt all day. They may trample pearls because they have no concept of value. They may even bite the hand that feeds them. But, they'd rather die than be possessed.

This leads me to the quick and humiliating conclusion that in our darkest moments we can be worse than pigs. They didn't even hesitate. When Legion's demons entered the herd, they voted instantly and unanimously to die rather than to live and be possessed by the demons. That must be a point in their favor. It is also an indicator of just how disgusting demons are. If a pig won't take you in, you're worse than garbage. The demons underestimated the pigs. I think that's kind of funny. Jesus didn't underestimate the pigs. He knew exactly what they would do.

7

SHEEP

I MUST CONFESS THAT SHEEP ARE not my favorite animals, although they seem to be the Lord's very favorite. There must be something wrong with me, I'm quite sure the Lord has excellent taste. Perhaps my years of working at the zoo have something to do with my attitude toward them. You see, among zookeepers caring for the sheep was considered as punishment when there were lions, tigers, bears, gorillas, rhinos, and a host of other more exotic animals to care for. The only value I ever noticed around the sheep was their willingness to subject themselves daily to eight hours of attention from unsupervised children. A part of me found it admirable that, despite the things that their little visitors did, the sheep never made an effort to retaliate. That kind of tolerance was rare around the zoo.

Thankfully, my personal association with sheep was infrequent. But there have been many others, long before me or my kind, whose jobs were to be full-time caregivers to sheep. We call them shepherds, and many great men of the Bible held that position at one time or another.

Abel was the first shepherd, as well as the first murder victim. Where were the sheep when he needed them? It should be no surprise to us that sheep aren't very useful in subduing an assailant. Jacob tended sheep most of his life. When he joined his son Joseph in Egypt, Joseph asked him not to mention that shepherding was the family business. In Egypt, shepherding was considered a menial task, and Joseph wanted his family to make a good impression on the Pharaoh.

What about Moses? When he fell from his lofty position as an Egyptian official and member of the royal family of Egypt, he found himself tending someone else's sheep. He had been in line for the throne of Egypt, but he had to run away to a despised country, Midian. There he spent the next forty years of his life as a shepherd. Such a radical shift in occupation had to be humiliating to a quasi-Egyptian who had been raised to think that shepherding was necessary but not a profession to which an educated person would aspire.

What about David? When he had been left alone in the field as a shepherd, he received a real put down. All the real men were in the army, and the army was assembled for battle with the great oppressors of the north. That's where real men belonged, on the front line, swords by their sides and spears in their hands, staring down the godless Philistines. But David was stuck with the sheep. When he finally got a chance to leave them and visit his brothers at the battle front, his oldest brother made fun of him and asked him who was watching the few little sheep while he was goofing off and trying to feel important with the warriors of Israel.

When I thought about all these shepherds, I came to realize that each Christian life has the potential for greatness, but that greatness is always preceded with lessons in humility. It might also be appropriate to say that the way to greatness is tending sheep. Jesus said, "Whoever can be trusted with very little can also be trusted with much" (Luke 16:10).

Maybe I should have volunteered for sheep care after all. Perhaps I would be a better person today for having done that more often. These great shepherds of the faith were, and they're a hard act to follow.

In John 10:11, Jesus tells us, "I am the good shepherd." He was willing to lay down His life for His sheep, namely, us. Jesus' journey was not unlike the journeys of Joseph or Moses, only more spectacular. For Joseph, he went from being a wealthy man's favorite son to slavery to the right hand of Pharaoh to delivering his family from the brink of ruin to its becoming the people of Israel. In the case of Moses, he went from the right hand of Pharaoh to shepherding to becoming the deliverer of his people and on to the right hand of God. The journey of Jesus was so much more. He left the right hand of the Father to become the good shepherd, a servant to sheep, and He saved the sheep from the destroyers around them, and He still watches over His flock. Nobody ever gave up more for humanity than Jesus did. He gave up His divinity to become human, and He gave His life that humanity could see how it could transcend the barrier that separated it from God. It is an incomparable deed. And He did it all for His sheep. But that's not the half of it. The more you learn about sheep, the more incomprehensible seems His love for us.

Sheep are mentioned more than five hundred times in Scripture, which is significantly greater than any other animal. In both the Old and New Testaments, sheep are the favorite analogy in describing people and their relationship to the Father. We are sheep. While being the sheep of our Lord's flock is indeed a blessing, I'm afraid it isn't much of a compliment.

I found ten negative and ten positive traits about sheep. Think of it as a good news/bad news situation. First, the bad news.

1. Sheep, of all the domestic animals, require the most care and supervision. Left to themselves, sheep have an unlimited capacity for getting into trouble. Shepherding is a day-and-night situation, a twenty-four-hour-a-day job. It is terrific to know that God never sleeps and watches over us day and night.

2. Sheep are compelled by mob instinct. Sheep take their cues from each other. If one sheep panics, they all panic. They tend to think as a group, not for themselves, so they just go with the flow, even if the flow is going the wrong way. Like sheep, we take our cues from each other more easily than taking them from God. The Scripture says:

We all, like sheep, have gone astray,
  each of us has turned to his own way.

Isaiah 53:6

3. Sheep are very susceptible to fear. The average sheep is a coward. One roar from a lion, one howl from a wolf, in fact, one loud noise of any kind can send a flock in every direction, away from the protection they enjoy under the care of the shepherd and the sheepdog. Their fear leaves them more vulnerable than ever to be destroyed, but they cannot help it for it is their nature. When confronted with danger, sheep panic, which is the response from a God-given survival mechanism. Before sheep were domesticated, with no shepherds around to protect them, fear would have had some survival value. Like all mammals faced with danger, the panic-stricken sheep gets a good shot of adrenalin to make it stronger to fight or flee. Because wild sheep don't have much going for them in the way of defense, running through rough terrain is their best chance to survive. Jesus' plea is for us not to be afraid because, under His care, there is no need to be afraid. He says, "Fear not. I am with you even unto the end of the world."

When I served at the Los Angeles Zoo, I saw what fear of pain and of death could do to a person. I saw it up close because that person's fear almost cost me my life.

Our zoo was a West Coast quarantine station for all animals destined for zoos in the Western United

States. The Fresno Zoo had ordered a black leopard, and it arrived at lunchtime on a day when our veterinarian had made lunch plans away from the zoo. Now our zoo had hired some fine men to offer veterinary care to the animals, but this man was not one of them, and I lamented being assigned to be his assistant. He was fresh out of school, arrogant, rich, pompous, selfish, given to tantrums and pouting, foolish, brash, and preoccupied with women. Other than that he was a real neat guy.

On this particular day, the doctor was almost out the door with Janice, our curator of mammals, when he was detained by the unloading of the leopard. It had to be done before lunch because 97° heat and an almost unventilated crate created a life-threatening situation for the leopard. When we examined the crate we were surprised to discover a structural problem. Usually, a crate used for shipping animals had a guillotine door at one end, which made it convenient for transferring the animal directly to its cage. But this crate did not have such a door. Instead, a square piece of plywood had been nailed onto the end to serve as a stationary door. It was also clear that the animal had been drugged, shoved into the crate, and the wooden door nailed securely in place. We guessed that everything had been done in a hurry.

The poor leopard had been confined for three days with no provision for fresh water, much less for having the crate cleaned. This was not unusual. Animal dealers, for the most part, rarely think beyond their profit margin. They certainly do not consider the welfare of the animal during the transaction.

Essentially, we were faced with the task of knocking off the end of a rectangular box to let a badly stressed leopard into its holding quarters. In my mind, that had to be done in two stages. First, we would have to loosen the end of the box slightly. Drag the box into the cage and then lock the cage. Second, we would finish knocking the end off the crate from outside the cage so that the leopard would not be in a position to attack us.

What seemed obvious to me was not at all obvious to our veterinarian. Why? Because it would take more time than he wanted to give to the task. He wanted to go to lunch.

He opened the sliding door to the holding cage and had us move the crate into position, as we would do with a normal crate. I asked what he planned to do, and he said, "Look, the leopard just wants out of the crate. So we'll each have a job to do." (Plan seemed flawless so far.) "I'll knock the front off the crate and step back quickly. Gary, you take this steel plate [he handed me a lightweight piece of aluminum, three feet wide and four feet tall], and when I step back, you cover the opening above the crate so the cat will think it can't get out. When the cat comes all the way out of the crate, Janice will slide the door shut, and we can all go to lunch."

Janice was a little arrogant around the animal keepers, mostly due to her academic achievements.

She had earned her doctorate by studying the evolution of frogs, which meant that she knew very little about mammals, especially leopards.

Given our circumstance, Janice had the most important job; it was essential that the door be closed behind the animal at just the right moment. If it wasn't, we would be trapped in close quarters with a species of animal that holds the distinction of having killed more zoo personal than any other animal.

I protested. "Doc, we could do this safer. We don't know whether the leopard is going to come out head first or tail first. If it comes out head first, we'll probably be fine, because it will most likely run into the empty cage. If it backs out, it will look at us and feel threatened. It might even try to attack us at that short distance. I'm not too keen on having a leopard in my face. Why not just drag the crate in the cage and knock the end off, and limit our chances of being attacked?"

I got a very dirty look for my efforts, and Janice said, "Gary, I think Doc knows what he is doing. Let's just get this done."

I was overruled. A keeper was assigned to beat on the crate, which provided incentive for the deadly cat to exit. Doc wet down the crate to cool it off, but he left the water running as he laid the hose down. We all had our assignments. Doc took a hammer and started hitting the end of the crate, which made the wooden door begin to loosen. From inside the crate, we heard a deep guttural roar that scared all of us witless.

Everyone jumped, then we all chuckled at our reactions. Someone said, "I meant to do that." My heart started pounding faster with every sound of the smack of the hammer against the crate. Within seconds, the time came for me to play my part. The plywood end was almost free, held by only a few remaining nails. Whack! The plywood flew off the end of the crate and into the cage. Doc threw himself out of the way, and I shoved the flimsy aluminum plate into the open area above the crate.

We waited. I was holding my breath and hoping beyond hope that I would soon see some whiskers and ears. Nothing happened for several seconds. The cat was hiding in the crate. The only ventilation was created by several half-inch holes drilled in the side of the crate. There was still no way to see which way the leopard was facing. Doc picked up the hose and forced the nozzle into one of the holes, hoping to squirt the cat. Another awesome roar shook the crate, louder now because one end of the crate was open. This was not the sound of a happy cat. Doc squirted water through the other holes. The cat reacted violently, and the crate rocked back and forth as the cat tried to avoid the spray. Then the worst possible thing happened.

The cat's twitching tail appeared.

"He's backing out," I yelled. "Get ready to shut that door." My heart was pounding so hard, I was sure it was visible. The hind quarters appeared slowly, and the leopard's beautiful black fur sparkled in the sun, highlighting the spots for which the leopard is known.

His muscular shoulders appeared, and I whispered, "Get ready Janice."

The head appeared, and the animal looked up at me, lowered his ears and roared. His eyes were filled with hatred, his body tense with rage. The cat was in the cage! But I couldn't understand why the door was not closed. I yelled, "Close the door!" That's when the leopard sprang toward my face and grabbed the aluminum panel, tearing it easily from my hands. He tossed it several feet in back of me. My face was three feet from the animal's face and *still* the door was not closed. I was fairly sure I was going to die, for there was no one there strong enough to pull me from the grasp of an adult male leopard. Its eyes were fixed on mine, unblinking, sinister.

I turned to yell one more time, "Shut the door now!" I was startled to see no one by the door. As it turned out, the well-educated Janice had run for it! I was vaguely conscious of the slamming of the cage room door then. To his credit, Doc didn't run, but he sprayed the leopard in the face with the water. It didn't do much for the angry cat's temper, but it did cause him to take his eyes off of me for a fraction of a second. I lunged for the sliding door and pulled it with all my strength. It was my only hope. The leopard reacted, but he was just a bit too late. The cunning predator slammed against the closing door and bounced off, hooking only the knuckle on my right hand with its claw. The hasp fell into place. I rolled away from the cage and laid on the wet concrete. I looked up at Doc,

---

who was still squirting the cat out of shear gut reaction. He dropped the hose and looked at me.

"You okay?" he asked sincerely.

I sat up and examined my hand, which now was bleeding a fair amount. "I think I'll make it. Where'd our help go?" I asked sarcastically. As it turned out, Janice was not the only one to bail out. The seasoned, veteran animal keeper had bailed out too and had actually fought his way through the outside door ahead of her to save his own skin.

I stood up and said, "That was a good thing you did with the hose. It saved the day, Doc, but don't ask me to work with those two in a dangerous situation again. They don't have what it takes. We almost got killed because of it."

He nodded.

I was really angry and would have done some first-class telling off except both of the deserters came back into the cage room ashamed and apologetic. Janice came in shaking her head as she said tearfully, "I'm so sorry, you guys. I lost it. Until this moment, I didn't know a human could be that afraid." She stared at the leopard that was now pacing nervously in its cage, stopping now and then to lower its ears and hiss. She was shaking in the 97° heat as though she were freezing. I didn't have the heart to rub it in. Besides, she had asked for forgiveness, and I was obliged. She was even more disturbed when she saw my hand, but I assured her that a penguin had once caused more damage and that I had come to expect scrapes, cuts, and bruises as part of the job. The truth was, I had experienced as much fear as I could ever want to and had merely reacted out of a sincere desire to preserve my own life. It was nothing to be proud of at all, but I was glad that I hadn't run away from the situation.

There are many times when fear can create panic, or cause a person to fight or strike out in anger, or it simply immobilizes. But all of us are afraid of something, real or imagined, and at times that fear shames us and humbles us. That is part of what it means to be a sheep.

4. Sheep are very timid. If you look in the dictionary under *sheep* you will see that it says, "meek, bashful or timid person." *Timid* in the same dictionary means, "shrinking from danger or risk; fearful. Lacking self-confidence; shy. Characterized by fear or shyness: a timid voice." You could add *reluctant* as a synonym. No matter how you look at it, timidity is not a good character trait. In sports, in business, or in battle, you don't want to deal with timid people.

A timid person risks nothing and so gains nothing. But let's not confuse timid with humble or meek. Humble or meek people would be willing to share their gifts with others on the basis that the gift being shared is of an enjoyable value to others. Timid people would be afraid to have their gifts evaluated or, even worse, think that they haven't any gifts at all. Timidity is not trying out of fear of failure or success.

5. Sheep are animals of low intelligence. I feel somewhat sensitive pointing out a sheep's intellectual shortcomings; it seems somewhat haughty to do so. I do take comfort in the thought that, should they somehow see or hear about my writing here, they would probably not understand it anyway. You see, their vocabulary is limited to one word: "Baa." They don't say "bah humbug" or "baa, baa, black sheep," just "baa."

I took care of a small flock of about thirty-five sheep while I was at the Los Angeles Zoo. Many times I attempted to engage them in conversation, only to be disappointed each time. "Good morning to all of you," I would say optimistically. "Baa," replied several in unison. "The weather is pleasant this time of year, wouldn't you say?" Again they would say, "Baa." Certainly, I do not expect sheep to actually speak with me about anything. It just seems to me that an animal whose verbal capacity is limited to one utterance is probably not the smartest of animals.

There is another aspect of the character of sheep that does not speak highly of their wisdom or intelligence. It is their mating behavior. When the females come into season, the males feel obligated to challenge other males for the right to mate. They stand several feet apart and run full speed at each other and butt heads. Mature males have major horns, like those you see on the Los Angeles Rams' football helmets. That kind of head butting has to do a number on each other's thinking capacity.

I stood and watched two males repeat this process over and over for about twenty minutes until one backed down. When they crashed into each other you could hear the sound a mile away. After crashing, they would just stand there pretending not to be in pain. The fact is, they were trembling with pain, their eyes unable to focus, just staring out into space. I always thought that this sequence would make a terrific aspirin commercial. They must have rammed each other twenty times during the "engagement." I was intrigued when the one finally gave up. The victor stood by the female for whom he had done battle. She winked at him. His reply, "Baa."

If sheep are intelligent, they would have, in the last several thousand years, figured out another mating behavior. They could draw straws, spit for distance, answer riddles, flip a coin, see who blinked first, or just ask the female to choose. Any method aside from head butting would be more intelligent. But that is the way they were designed by God.

6. Sheep are very destructive. Sheep have the very bad habit of being very hard on the pasture. When they graze, they don't trim the grasses they eat. They bite down and pull up, removing the roots, stems and all. This, of course, prevents the grass from growing back. Left to themselves, sheep would seldom move on to "greener pastures" before they had completely damaged the one they're in. They need a shepherd who will keep them moving so that they simply thin out areas and not destroy them completely.

It was this destructive habit that set off the range wars between cattle ranchers and sheep herders in the Western United States late in the last century. The cattlemen were livid when they came upon vast areas of denuded grazing land. The historical novelist James Michener, in his epic novel *Centennial*, gives a fascinating characterization of the problems and enmity between the cattle barons and sheep ranchers in a chapter entitled "The Smell of Sheep." The destruction of grazing land was an understandable frustration for the cattlemen.

7. **Sheep are very stubborn.** Sheep herding is no walk in the park for a shepherd. Once sheep have found a spot to graze, they are quite content to lay it to waste. Were it not for sheepdogs nipping at their heels, they would be difficult to move, because sheep are not only stubborn, they're greedy. Where their food source is plentiful, you will find sheep eating for the future, growing fat beyond both necessity and reason. This year at the county fair in Los Angeles I watched four sheep, each intent on eating the last flake of alfalfa hay as it was laid out for them. Each sheep was not only several pounds overweight, each was bloated and looked as if it were going to burst. Yet it was obvious that none of the four were about to give the advantage of an extra bite to the others. The pushing and shoving was not unlike what we commonly see in the malls during an after-Christmas sale.

Sheep may be timid in the face of danger, but they are extremely selfish and bold with each other. They are typically stubborn and greedy. That's why the Book of Isaiah says, "The earth lies polluted under its inhabitants" (Isa. 24:5 RSV); among other things to our shame, we have exploited the earth in the same way that sheep overgraze a pasture, stubbornly refusing to stop. At this juncture, we are worse than sheep, because we realize what we are doing, but we allow these problems to compound and hope that our future generations will solve them.

8. Sheep have a tendency to wander off. Sheep are forever getting lost. Their lack of focus is a great source of concern, because they allow the herd to go on without them while they dally. Sometimes it's a matter of sleeping when they ought to be on the move with the herd. Sometimes it's a matter of looking for something they can enjoy on their own without having to share it with another sheep. For whatever reason, sheep go astray, and that's bad, because there is no protection apart from the herd. This is true of humans also. This trait was used by Isaiah when he wrote, "All we like sheep have gone astray, we have turned every one to his own way" (Isa. 53:6 RSV). Once lost, a sheep must be found by someone else because, although it could rejoin the herd by following it, that idea never seems to occur to the sheep.

9. Sheep are very vulnerable to predators. Among animals, sheep are wimps. They are weak, slow, stupid, and defenseless. They lean toward panic when confronted. Even if they didn't panic, they would be overmatched by any predator. They are to the animal world what Barney Fife was to law enforcement. Jesus must have frightened His disciples when He said in Matthew, "Behold, I send you out as sheep in the midst of wolves; so be wise as serpents and innocent as doves" (Matt. 10:16 RSV). Sheep in the midst of wolves would certainly not last for long. With the right tactics, we could hold our own until the shepherd returns. Under our own power we could never survive among the wolves. Our only salvation is to live by the power of the Holy Spirit within us and under His protection. Still, few sheep ever use the power they have and are easily defeated when confronted by a true predator.

10. Sheep have an incredible ability to get dirty. If your mental image of a sheep is that of a fluffy puff of white with legs and a head, you are thinking of a sheep freshly sheared and cleaned up for judging at the local county fair. That sheep has not been in a pasture with a herd but in a stall filled with fresh straw, which is changed several times daily. After the fair and all the special care, it will begin to get dirty and take on a color you would never paint your house or car.

Sheepskin is full of an oil called lanolin. Lanolin comes through the skin and coats the wool. It conditions the wool so that the animal will stay warm in cold weather, but the oily wool is one of the most effective dirt-catching devices known to man. Every time a sheep lays down, grass, dirt, burrs, dust, and everything imaginable clings to its coat. Sheep are huge walking velcro strips. They turn every shade of gray and brown imaginable. If you want to smell something unique, take a whiff of a herd of sheep after an afternoon rain. That will both wake you up and clear your senses.

Sheep get dirty and stay that way until someone cleans them up. That's true of us also. We cannot clean ourselves—but God can. The effect of our asking for God's forgiveness is laid out in Isaiah, "Come now, let us reason together, says the LORD: though your sins are like scarlet, they shall be as white as snow" (Isa. 1:18 RSV).

We are just like sheep. As time passes we get dirty. We say the wrong thing, do the wrong thing, want the wrong thing until it becomes obvious we need a good cleaning. A bath is the easiest thing in the world. For us, it happens if we are simply willing to confess our sins to God and ask Him to forgive us.

Now as negative as some of these things are about sheep, it would be unfair to generate the impression that they are valueless. There are ten positive things I'd like to point out about sheep.

1. Sheep are clearly God's favorite animals. Hands down, no contest. In a world filled with majestic animals like lions, horses, and eagles, the Lord chose sheep. And there isn't a better metaphor in Scripture for our relationship to God. *We* are his sheep.

The Scripture also mentions lambs—the pure, clean, young sheep. It was the greatest compliment in all of Scripture when Jesus was called the Lamb of God:

> The next day he [John the Baptist] saw Jesus coming toward him, and said, "Behold, the Lamb of God, who takes away the sin of the world!"
>
> *John 1:29 RSV*

In Revelation, we read:

> Worthy is the Lamb who was slain, to receive power and wealth and wisdom and might and honor and glory and blessing!
>
> *Revelation 5:12 RSV*

Jesus was the valued Son of the living God. And by our relationship to Him, we become valued children of God. In spite of the negative traits of sheep discussed above, which also seem to fit us snugly, Jesus—the good shepherd—willingly chose to give His life for His sheep.

> I am the good shepherd. The good shepherd lays down his life for the sheep. He who is a hireling and not a shepherd, whose own the sheep are not, sees the wolf coming and leaves the sheep and flees; and the wolf snatches them and scatters them. He flees because he is a hireling and cares nothing for the sheep. I am the good shepherd; I know my own and my own

know me, as the Father knows me and I know the
Father; and I lay down my life for the sheep. And I
have other sheep, that are not of the fold; I must bring
them also, and they will heed my voice. So there shall
be one flock, one shepherd. For this reason the Father
loves me, that I lay down my life, that I may take it
again.

John 10:11–18 RSV

How can I be sure sheep are His favorite animals?
I am one of His sheep, and He was willing to die for
me. If you belong to Christ, and even if you don't, it is
still true that He was willing to die for you and did.
Nothing you have ever done nor anything anyone else
has ever done declares our value in God's eyes more
undeniably. At that historic moment, Jesus laid down
His life on the cross for His sheep, and we became
priceless. Even the least of Christ's sheep is of more
value than anything else on earth, and the same price
was paid for all of us.

You are not your own; you were bought with a
price. So glorify God in your body.

1 Corinthians 6:19–20 RSV

2. Sheep have *horns*. The word *horn* has two
meanings. It can mean simply a projection of
glutinated hair on the head of a hoofed animal, or it
can mean a musical instrument, like a trumpet.
"Horn" was applied to the trumpet out of the use of a

ram's horn as a musical instrument. In truth, the first trumpets were rams horns. When Joshua was told to march the armies of Israel to Jericho and attack, he probably wondered how they were going to overcome the mighty walls that surrounded the city.

> Thus shall you do for six days. And seven priests shall bear seven trumpets of rams' horns before the ark; and on the seventh day you shall march around the city seven times, the priests blowing the trumpets. And when they make a long blast with the ram's horn, as soon as you hear the sound of the trumpet, then all the people shall shout with a great shout; and the wall of the city will fall down flat, and the people will go up every man straight before him.
>
> *Joshua 6:4–5* RSV

Those ram's horns/trumpets were announcing the presence of the Lord. They were instruments of praise. They were part of a mighty victory. The trumpet sound was made with a ram's horn. That means that sheep can literally be instruments of praise. We, being His sheep, also have that capability. We can announce His coming and His majesty. And indeed it is our responsibility to do just that. We are charged with the mission to announce to everyone we meet that the Lord has affected our lives radically and that He is able to address their needs and heal their wounds also. The difference between sheep and us on this point is that we don't have to lose anything to announce the gospel. Our "horn" is not detached so that another can use it to generate the notes of the word of the Lord. Our horn is an intrinsic part of us, and we need to use it ourselves so that others can be drawn into the fold as well.

3. Sheep are the favorite meat in the Middle East. When making shishkabob in the Middle East, there is only one choice of meat—sheep. Sheep meat feeds the hungry. When Jesus commanded His disciples to drink of His blood and eat of His flesh, He was not being literal; He was telling them to fill up on His teachings, His being, and His character. He was speaking as the sacrificial lamb, seeking to satisfy our real needs with His love. And His love gives us love to share with others. Although God's love would be enough for anyone, He blesses us by allowing us to find love and affection, spiritual knowledge, experience, guidance, and support from those around us. These kinds of things complete our nourishment and fill us with the peace and security of living under the care of the Good Shepherd.

4. Sheep give milk. Sheep can quench thirst. Sheep's milk is commonplace in the Middle East. As sheep, we can also quench thirst. We can do it both in the physical sense as well as the spiritual sense as we are commanded to give a cup of water unto the least of those we meet.

The woman at the well was told by Jesus that He could give her water of a kind that would quench her thirst forever. We can do that also, because we can offer the saving life of Jesus to others. Liquids are more essential to life than food. While we can go for as long as thirty days without food, we could only last as long as three to five days without water. As His sheep, we have both the sincere milk of the Word and the water of life to offer to a thirsty world.

5. Sheepskins are used for shelter and clothing. The nomadic shepherds of the Middle East lived in tents. They were sheltered from the desert sun, harsh winds, and vicious sand and dust storms. They also made jackets and vests for protective covering and simple clothing. Housing and clothing are simple, basic needs that all of us share. Just as sheep have the potential to provide these things for us, we can provide these things for others.

6. Sheep give us wool. Some would say that the primary mission of sheep is the generation of wool. After all, the animals grow a thick coat of wool regularly. That thick wool is then cut off and used to produce clothing. Wool serves two purposes: to keep us warm and to cool us off. Being light in color, wool mostly reflects heat while its substance insulates us from the cold. And extreme heat and cold are two things that we avoid. In either extremity, heat and cold become life threatening.

Joseph, the son of Jacob, was given a valuable coat made of wool as a sign of his father's love and favor. And it was the only proof his brothers could offer their father of Joseph's "death." Similarly, the only known possession of Jesus was a wool robe. It had kept Him warm and protected Him from the sun. Jesus' robe must have been a good garment because the Roman soldiers responsible for overseeing the crucifixion gambled for it. To this day, coats and sweaters made from sheepskin and wool are not only protective, they are also prized and expensive clothing.

7. Sheep were used as a symbol for Christ in the Old Testament sacrificial system. The first sheep was sacrificed by Abel, Adam and Eve's son:

> Now Abel was a keeper of the sheep, and Cain a tiller of the ground. In the course of time Cain brought to the LORD an offering of the fruit of the ground, and Abel brought of the firstlings of his flock and of their fat portions. And the LORD had regard for Abel and his offering, but for Cain and for his offering he had no regard.
>
> *Genesis 4:2–5 RSV*

We are told nothing about how sacrifice was originally instituted, but some things seem to present themselves as obvious. Sacrifice became a way that we could show respect to God; we gave the Lord the best of what we had to offer. Even in this first story of sacrifice, it is evident that God wanted two things. He wanted Cain and Abel to be willing to trust Him for a blessing by giving Him the very best of what they had. Also, He wanted them to do it with a good attitude. The first shepherd, Abel, did just that, and he found favor with God.

By Genesis 22, in the story of Abraham, God makes it clear that human sacrifice is never required and that He alone will provide the sacrifice for salvation. God demanded the best Abraham had to offer, his son Isaac. And Abraham was willing to give him up, believing that God would resurrect him. God knew that killing Isaac wouldn't do any good, because Isaac, as much as Abraham loved him, was not perfect. His sacrifice would be an exercise in futility. God would instead give His Son, Jesus, who was perfect, and that would be the last, the final sacrifice on mankind's behalf.

After these things God tested Abraham, and said to him, "Abraham!" And he said, "Here am I." He said, "Take your son, your only son Isaac, whom you love, and go to the land of Moriah, and offer him there as a burnt offering upon one of the mountains of which I shall tell you." So Abraham rose early in the morning, saddled his ass, and took two of his young men with him, and his son Isaac; and he cut the wood for the burnt offering, and arose and went to the place of which God had told him. On the third day Abraham lifted up his eyes and saw the place afar off. Then Abraham said to his young men, "Stay here with the ass; I and the lad will go yonder and worship, and come again to you." And Abraham took the wood of the burnt offering, and laid it on Isaac his son; and he took in his hand the fire and the knife. So they went both of them together. And Isaac said to his father Abraham, "My Father!" And he said, "Here am I, my son." He said, "Behold the fire and the wood; but where is the lamb for a burnt offering?" Abraham said, "God will provide himself the lamb for a burnt offering, my son." So they went both of them together.

When they came to the place of which God had told him, Abraham built an altar there, and laid the wood in order, and bound Isaac his son, and laid him upon the altar, upon the wood. Then Abraham put forth his hand, and took the knife to slay his son. But the angel of the Lord called to him from heaven, and said, "Abraham, Abraham!" And he said, "Here am I." He said, "Do not lay your hand on the lad or do anything to him; for now I know that you fear God, seeing you have not withheld your son, your only son, from me." And Abraham lifted his eyes and looked, and behold, behind him was a ram, caught in a thicket by his horns; and Abraham went and took the ram, and offered it up as a burnt offering instead of his son. So Abraham called the name of the place The Lord will provide; as it is said to this day, "On the mount of the Lord it shall be provided."

Genesis 22:1–14

Abraham exhibited ultimate obediance to the will and call of God. And his unbending trust was rewarded, because his faith was in God.

Perhaps the greatest example of the sacrifice as a symbol of God's protection is found in Exodus 12. God decided to bring the worst of all plagues on the Egyptians. Because Pharaoh refused to let His people go, He decided to kill all of Egypt's firstborn, human or animal. He gave the Jews specific instructions so that they might avoid the curse. He told the Jews to sacrifice unblemished lambs and then smear its blood on the doorposts and lintels of their homes. The blood would be a sign of obedience and faith in God's commands, and it would protect the home from the curse. They were also told to eat these sacrificial lambs, not just parts of them, but they were to be roasted whole. Any leftovers had to be burned by morning. Israel did as they were commanded, and when the Lord passed over, He sent an awesome creature or angel called the destroyer into all of the unprotected homes and wiped out the firstborn Egyptians. This event is, to this day, considered to be the most important in Jewish history. The Jews were delivered by the blood of the Passover lambs.

When you put these pictures together, you see previews of coming attractions. Sacrifice was a symbol from the beginning. The sacrifice had to be the best you had to offer, without blemish, presented with unselfish love. So Jesus, the only begotten Son of God, perfect and without blemish, became the sacrifice for an imperfect mankind.

John the Baptist said: "Behold the Lamb of God which takes away the sins of the world." Jesus is the permanent Passover Lamb. We who have the Son, have life. Those without the Son don't have life and are set to run headlong into the wrath of God. Nowadays, the blood of the Lamb of God protects us. All we have to do is to accept Him. As Jesus put it, "Drink of my blood and eat of my flesh," just like the Passover lambs. Christ was the final sacrifice because after Christ there was nothing more to be given that would make a difference.

The Lord gave a singular honor to sheep when they came to be symbols of Christ. Since the time of Christ, there has never been, nor could there be, a sacrifice as powerful.

8. Sheep fertilize the earth wherever they go. Sheep prepare the earth for planting. In one sense, they give back a portion of what they have taken as they graze. Soil preparation is essential to plant growth. We can do something similar by living our lives in Christ the way we ought to live them. Preparing soil for the planting of our faith can be as simple as keeping our yard decent so the neighborhood is prettier because we are there. We can work without complaining, or just work hard without cutting corners. We can have a great attitude when things aren't fair. We can show interest in others and do something besides moan on their behalf. We can keep our priorities straight: our God, our families, our friends, our careers. If we are living like the salt of the earth we were meant to be, we will make the world around us a better place. We will prepare the soil for planting just as sheep prepare their pastures.

9. Sheep plant the seeds that will ensure future pastures. In Bible times, sheep were instrumental in planting seeds. During the harvest, wheat seeds were knocked from the wheat stalks onto the ground. They would lay on the surface and be eaten by the birds except that shepherds would bring their flocks into the now-harvested field. The pointed cloven hooves of the sheep would make holes one-half to one-inch deep, and the seeds would be pressed into the ground. In the push and shove of the herd, another sheep would cover the seeds with dirt, thus completing the planting of the seed. Pretty neat, isn't it? When it comes to making a natural system that takes care of itself, God is the master planner. Seed planting is one of our main responsibilites as part of His flock. God's Word tells us that He brings the increase to what we have sown and planted in our work. The harvest is the kingdom of God.

10. Many parts of a sheep can be used as tools. Bones can be made into sewing needles and used for scraping and shaping devices. Intestines can be made into strings for musical instruments. We can be instruments of His mercy and more effective than any sheep that ever lived. What being His sheep means more than anything is that we have unlimited potential. Once in His flock, even our weaknesses become strengths.

We require more care than any other animal and He loves to give us that care. We have a mob instinct, but when that is channeled it can become a great show of unity. We are subject to fear, but He gives us courage and the peace that surpasses all our understanding. We are also timid, but He makes us brave. All of us have a tendency to wander off now and then, but our Shepherd always finds us. He forgives us and cleans us so that we are ever presentable to God the Father. I am so thankful that I am His and He is mine.

8

RAVENS

Y OU MIGHT FIND IT INTERESTING to note that ravens are more responsible for the writing of this book than any of the other animals about which I have written. You see, I was on my way to work one morning when I happened to tune in one of my favorite Bible teachers on the radio. He was speaking about Elijah, expounding on the passage in 1 Kings 17 where Elijah stayed near the Brook of Cherith and was fed by the ravens. The speaker's premise concerned God's servants taking time to enjoy rest and recuperation when they were broken and weary. Much of what he was saying was true; God's servants do require rest and relaxation, just like everyone else. What bothered me was his interpretation of the atmosphere of Elijah's R&R.

The speaker described the incident as a wonderful opportunity for Elijah to collect his thoughts and reflect on and enjoy the beautiful outdoors. His portrayal was enthusiastic and made it sound like Elijah had the equivalent of an all-expense paid vacation to the Israeli Ritz Carlton. If you read the passage for yourself, you are likely to agree with the speaker and see Elijah luxuriating in comfortable surroundings.

However, there are five important things that change the complexion of the passage, making the R&R theory impossible.

First, allow me to sketch in a little background. Israel had the misfortune of having Ahab as her king. He reigned for twenty-two years and became known as one of the most evil kings in Israel's history. During his reign of unholiness, thousands of Israel's babies were sacrificed to the false gods of the people around Israel and adulterers, murderers, and thieves were as numerous as periods in the dictionary.

The Scripture says, "Ahab son of Omri did more evil in the eyes of the LORD than any of those before him" (1 Kings 16:30). Can you imagine being named as the new reigning champion of evil? And then Ahab married Jezebel, the daughter of Ethbaal king of the Sidonians. Ahab followed along with his wife in serving and worshiping Baal. "So he erected an altar for Baal in the house of Baal, which he built in Samaria. . . . Thus Ahab did more to provoke the LORD God of Israel than all the kings of Israel who were before him" (1 Kings 16:32–33 NASB). In short order, God became angry with the people's willing participation along with their monarchs in these unspeakable acts of evil. So He caused a severe drought to come upon the land and He announced through his prophet, Elijah, that He was sending this drought.

The Lord was ready to set the stage for something, but to accomplish it, He had to also prepare His prophet. Turning to the Scripture, we read that Elijah had a small journey to make:

Then the word of the LORD came to Elijah: "Leave here, turn eastward and hide in the Kerith Ravine, east of the Jordan. You will drink from the brook, and I have ordered the ravens to feed you there."

So he did what the LORD had told him. He went to Kerith Ravine, east of the Jordan, and stayed there. The ravens brought him bread and meat in the morning and bread and meat in the evening, and he drank from the brook. Some time later the brook dried up because there had been no rain in the land.

1 Kings 17:2–7

Why was this not R&R? For one thing, Elijah was asked to hide. While Elijah was there, he was evidently fearful that his life might end at any time. Perhaps he was afraid that Ahab would blame him for the drought that had laid seige to these once-fertile lands.

Second, he was alone for a long time. It must have been a considerable amount of time, I think, because the brook had time to dry up. We may assume, then, that he was lonely.

Third, he was *not* in a beautiful canyon by a majestic river. Rather, he was in a shallow ravine next to a small brook. Can you think of a famous national ravine that people camp around for the pleasure of enjoying nature?

Elijah's only sustenance was the courtesy of a band of ravens. The food was carried to him and dropped at his feet. Now that sounds great, but consider this: Ravens were unclean birds. In fact, in Leviticus

11:13–15, the Lord went so far as to declare them to be detestable birds. Ravens are scavengers, therefore they and anything they touch is also unclean. They'll eat just about anything, dead and decaying meat, rodents, insects, and rotten garbage. They are without taste and are absolutely disgusting. If that weren't enough, it was a well-known fact that ravens store their food in cow dung in order to prevent it from freezing in the winter. They also sift through the cow dung searching for tasty dung beetles.

I'm absolutely sure that Elijah's stomach turned when the first delivery raven arrived. Knowing their habits, he would have wondered where that raven's beak had been just prior to its visit with the food. He may also have known that ravens have an interesting relationship with wolves. Some people believe that ravens have a way of communicating the whereabouts of live food to wolves. Then the ravens get to eat the wolves' leftovers, which generally is a favorite food of theirs anyway.

Shortly before Elijah arrived, the drought struck. The brook in the Kerith Ravine was small to begin with, so even that began to shrink away as time passed. The water would have been warm. It would also have been a little rusty due to the high iron content of the area, and it would have been filled with algae and small organisms that can make your insides feel as if they are being ravaged by a little war of germs. Finally, the brook dried up, and Elijah was commanded to "Go at once to Zarephath of Sidon and

---

stay there. I have commanded a widow in that place to supply you with food" (verse 9).

This was no holiday in the tropics for Elijah by any measure of one's imagination. He was hiding for his life, and he was alone. He found himself in a lackluster ravine during a fearsome drought, where he lived on two meals a day and mucky water. The diet never varied, just bread and meat delivered by some biblically detestable birds which he knew were ritually unclean to his God. When the water dried up, he was sent to sponge off of a poverty-stricken, single-parent widow. This is nobody's idea of Camp Fun.

But God was giving Elijah a course in advanced humility to His powerful and sometimes haughty prophet. God was saying, "Elijah, I'll protect you and care for you, but I will do it on My terms in My time, and by My methods." God has the right to do that, you know, to guide us through humility toward Christian maturity. Throughout the course of 1 Kings 17:1– 24, Elijah received his doctorate in humility and sovereignty.

Now that is the way I interpreted the passage in 1 Kings 17, and that is what gave birth to the idea of this book. There is so much more depth to the story when the ways and habits of these unusual birds are clearly explained. I hope it is helpful to you.

It may interest you to know that ravens are considered to be the most intelligent of all the birds. They are problem solvers. Unfortunately, they will most likely remain unpopular because of our pattern of associating them with horror, filth, and evil. Alfred Hitchcock's film, *The Birds,* has made them out to be veritable man killers. Edgar Allen's Poe's poem, "The Raven," drapes them with malice and foreboding. And then in Luke we read:

> Consider the ravens: They do not sow or reap, they have no storeroom or barn; yet God feeds them. And how much more valuable you are than birds!
>
> *Luke 12:24*

Their own sickening habits continue to remind us that they are undesirables among animals. Yet it helps me to remember that God made them that way and cares for them still. How wonderful is our God.

9

EAGLES

WHEN YOU WORK AT A ZOO, you quickly find that you
need a particularly good reason to cage majestic animals for public display. If that justification isn't obvious, you feel guilty and depressed as you go about
your work. Fortunately, in most cases, sufficient reasons exist. For example, a zoo's environment protects
the population of rare and endangered animals by
providing a safe haven for them. For animals that
could be threatened in the wild, a zoo offers medical
help, a balanced diet, and protection from natural
predators. Of equal importance is a zoo's responsibility for bringing the wonders of the animal kingdom to
the attention of humankind. Children and adults in
urban or rural communities might spend a lifetime
and never witness the beauty and mystery of these
animals. For those reasons, I could understand and
actively participate in the care of captive animals, with
one exception. Regal, noble, majestic eagles do not
belong in cages.

The Greek word for eagle is *aetos,* which means to
blow as the wind or to become one with the wind.
Animals who belong with the wind should not be

expected to sit on perches all day and do nothing but look back at people looking at them. The thought of that saddens me more than I can say.

One of my greatest memories occurred on a late June day at Forest Home Christian Conference Center in Forest Falls, California. I had just led a group of a hundred people on a nature walk through a beautiful box canyon, nestled some five thousand feet in the heart of the San Bernadino Mountains. I was standing on a mile-high ridge overlooking the creek that snakes through the picturesque campground, when a movement to my left caught my attention. Soaring at eye level, only thirty feet from where I was standing, was a Golden Eagle. It was very large, so I judged her to be a female. She slowed, almost stopping in mid-air. She was literally riding the wind, adjusting to every variance of its velocity and swirling thermals, all the while studying me. Our eyes met. I didn't move a muscle. I remember thinking, *God has blessed me by allowing me to witness such a wonder so close at hand.* For several moments, I was frozen in time, wishing this sweet communion might last a little longer for I was sure I might never enjoy a moment like this again.

I was amazed at the eagle's control. Then in a moment, she veered off and swooped downward to pick up speed. She was soaring down the canyon at more than sixty miles per hour. I watched until she was out of sight.

As my eyes followed her in flight, my mind was flooded with all the amazing things that I had learned

about Golden Eagles while working at the zoo. I knew
that they could attain speeds in excess of a hundred
miles per hour in a dive. I remembered that they could
maintain those incredible speeds to the point of impact
while maintaining their focus on the object upon
which they were diving. They are so coordinated they
can avoid mid-air collisions at that speed and actually
drag just one-eighth of an inch of talon across the back
of another bird, sending it spiraling to the ground in
shock. Sometimes they close their talons, as if making
a fist, to bash their prey as they swoop by.

I have two close friends, both jet pilots, who have
seen Golden Eagles in flight above fifteen thousand
feet. The eagles court at these great heights. When they
are ready to mate, the male locks talons with the female, and they freefall several thousand feet, mating
as they fall. Eagles are one of the few species of animals that bond for life.

As my newfound eagle-friend in the Forest Falls
canyon became little more than a speck in the distance,
I remembered another amazing eagle characteristic.
Eagles have better than average vision. I knew that
even at that tremendous distance, she was seeing me
with far greater clarity than I was seeing her. You and I
have some two hundred thousand visual receptors per
square centimeter in our eyes; eagles have 1.6 million
receptors per square centimeter. That gives them
incredibly high visual resolution.

To illustrate, imagine sitting in the last row of the
Los Angeles Coliseum. With the help of binoculars, a

person might accurately follow the action of a football contest. However, from that same distance, an eagle could distinguish every individual blade of grass on the playing field. Eagles could read three-inch high letters on a billboard one mile away, or they could see small fish jumping out of the water five miles out to sea. Incredible!

Another special quality of eagles is their remarkable strength. An eagle weighing about twenty pounds would have enough strength in its talons to break both of the bones in a man's forearm by merely grasping it firmly. Any small, unsuspecting prey would surely perish from that kind of power, as the specially designed talons on the mighty eagle's claws would also pierce the flesh of the doomed animal.

By the way, the eagle's talons are of special importance, also. While assisting Dr. Charles Sedgwick, our zoo's veterinarian, I learned that surgical needles were modeled after eagles' talons. They are specially crafted to pierce flesh, not tear it. So we who have had to have cuts sutured or surgeries performed should be grateful for God having allowed us to recognize yet another useful application of His handiwork.

Yes, there are many reasons to admire this regal fowl that is our nation's symbol for independence. Everything about an eagle cries out freedom and majesty. You may know about the long-ago discussion concerning the selection of the eagle as our national symbol. Benjamin Franklin felt that we would do well to select the feathered friend who had helped the Pilgrims through that first harsh winter near Plymouth Rock. He suggested that we honor the wild turkey, arguing that the eagle was hardly more than a carrion eater and not nearly as intelligent as the wild turkey. But it was to no avail. Just about everyone else liked the Bald Eagle. Aren't we glad they did? Imagine this: the English lion, the Russian bear, the African leopard, and the American turkey. There is definitely something wrong with that picture!

Had Franklin taken more of a biblical stance, citing Leviticus, he might have encouraged a few more of our forefathers to "talk turkey." Would you have changed your vote after hearing this:

> These are the birds you are to detest and not eat because they are detestable: The eagle, the vulture, the black vulture.
>
> *Leviticus 11:13*

That is not exactly complimentary. But a closer inspection leads us to believe the writer was actually expressing concern for Israel's dietary matters. Quite frankly, I cannot imagine eating the meat of an eagle anyway, can you?

Every other biblical mention of eagles deals with the animal's finer qualities and strengths. Perhaps one of these more familiar verses holds a special meaning for you.

In the Book of Exodus we find eagles used as a

symbol for the deliverance of God's people.

> You yourselves have seen what I did to the
> Egyptians, and how I bore you on eagles' wings and
> brought you to Myself.
>
> *Exodus 19:4 NASB*

What a tribute. Of the nearly ten thousand species of birds, God chose eagles' wings as the illustration of deliverance for His people Israel. He brought them to Himself. You remember *aetos*, to blow with the wind, become one with the wind? The eagle was the representation of the wind. The wind is God's Spirit.

Think about the biblical symbols for the Holy Spirit. In the Old Testament we see God's power associated with the strengths of His awesome and beautiful creatures, as was the case with that passage in Exodus. In the New Testament, the writers often compared the mighty Spirit of God with a dove, or a strong wind, or with fire. In Acts, Luke describes the coming of the Holy Spirit.

> When the day of Pentecost came, they were all
> together in one place. Suddenly a sound like the
> blowing of a violent wind came from heaven and
> filled the whole house where they were sitting. They
> saw what seemed to be tongues of fire that separated
> and came to rest on each of them. All of them were
> filled with the Holy Spirit and began to speak in
> tongues as the Spirit enabled them.
>
> *Acts 2:1–4*

Also, in the Gospel of John, we read:

> The wind blows where it wishes and you hear the
> sound of it, but do not know where it comes from and
> where it is going; so [it is] with one who is born of the
> Spirit.

John 3:8 NASB

From the deliverance of God's people from the
land of Egypt, to the day of Pentecost and the anoint-
ing of the Holy Spirit, on the wings of eagles to the
rush of a mighty wind, God was about the business of
caring for His people.

Another passage in Deuteronomy is a clear example of that special kind of caring. And once again
the illustration is that of an eagle.

> Like an eagle that stirs up its nest
>   and hovers over its young,
> that spreads its wings to catch them
>   and carries them on its pinions.

Deuteronomy 32:11

Unfortunately, this description must be of an eagle
that is now extinct. For of the twelve species of eagles
that live in Israel, there is not one that exhibits the
behaviors mentioned in this passage. Sadly, Israel is
the most ecologically depleted county in the world
and many animals no longer exist that once lived there
in abundance.

Even so, we can explore a wonderful parental object lesson. The eagle in this passage does what all parents are supposed to do. It teaches, motivates, protects, and supports its young.

The eagle provokes or stirs up its young every time it lands on the nest. Landing on the nest is the biological signal given to baby birds that it's time to eat. The hungrier they are, the more stirred they are.

By landing and leaving time and again, the eagle is modeling important behaviors and hoping its young are motivated to follow. It becomes a matter of life and death for all concerned that the young learn to fly and hunt, for at a certain point, the parent eagles can no longer keep up with the demands of feeding their young.

Teaching occurs when the mother hovers over the nest. The young, who have been beating their wings furiously for days, practicing flight, imitate what they have seen demonstrated repeatedly—how to fly, hover, take off, and land. The hunger of the babies finally causes them to rise above their fear of falling. It becomes a do-or-die situation, for everyone has to leave the nest sometime.

When this mother catches her babies on her wings, she is demonstrating protection. When she carries them, that's support. It's what parents do. If we didn't support our children and believe in them, they wouldn't do nearly as well.

For eagles, this entire process of raising their young takes about three and a half months. For the hummingbird—only eighteen days. Snakes are on their own from the first day. We human parents must wait from eighteen to twenty-five years (and some longer) to enjoy the fruits of our efforts. (Then we discover that we never really finish raising our kids.)

An eagle's parenting techniques are an integral part of its complex nature. But one of the most notable qualities of eagles is their extraordinary ability to fly. The Bible gives us one of the most beautiful tributes ever written. This well-known passage is found in Isaiah 40:

> Do you not know?
>   Have you not heard?
> The LORD is the everlasting God,
>   the Creator of the ends of the earth.
> He will not grow tired or weary,
>   and His understanding no one can fathom.
> He gives strength to the weary
>   and increases the power of the weak.
> Even youths grow tired and weary,
>   and young men stumble and fall;
> but those who hope in the LORD
>   will renew their strength.
> They will soar on wings like eagles;
>   they will run and not grow weary,
>   they will walk and not be faint.
>
> *Isaiah 40:28–31*

When eagles soar, it is not by their own strength. They merely extend their mighty wings and are lifted by the rising currents of air. They make themselves available to the wind in much the same way that God wishes us to make ourselves available to His strength and His Spirit, so that we may "soar on wings like eagles."

God wants us to place our trust in Him, and He will strengthen us. His strength is made perfect because of our weakness. He never meant for us to live life on our own. He meant that we should be willing and trusting, like the eagle whose ability to fly is only as great as the wind that carries it. Our strength is in God. How utterly amazing!

As the writer of the Proverbs considered:

> There are three things that are too amazing
> for me,
> four that I do not understand:
> the way of an eagle in the sky,
> the way of a snake on a rock,
> the way of a ship on the high seas,
> and the way of a man with a maiden.
>
> *Proverbs 30:18–19*

"The way of an eagle in the sky," negotiating the mighty winds, soaring to incredible heights, covering great distances. The mystery of an eagle's flight is as beautiful and wonderful as the Lord's way with His people. *Aetos*, to blow with the wind, to be one with the wind, is what God was trying to tell us in Isaiah 40. God wants us to be willing to go where the wind of His Spirit takes us, wherever that may be.

178

10

WOLVES

OF ALL THE PREDATORS THAT GOD created, wolves are by far the most persistent. Not even the shrew, who is the most tenacious, will stay with the hunt like wolves. The Cape hunting dogs of Africa, for example, are not nearly as large or as formidable as wolves, but they equal wolves in endurance. In general, it is characteristic of all canines that they persist.

A large wolf may weigh in excess of 160 pounds. As some studies have shown, a wolf can jog 45 miles a day on an average hunt. A group of wolves in Siberia were once observed traveling 125 miles in one day. They seem tireless as they wear down their prey.

Besides endurance, a wolf is also capable of exerting great strength. It can bite through the back leg of a horse and crunch the bone with its powerful jaws. The measure of that tremendous force is an unbelievable 1,500 pounds per square inch. Compare that with a German Shepherd's 750 pounds per square inch, and a wolf's biting power seems awesome indeed.

In spite of the wolf's considerable potential against larger prey, it will more often concentrate on defenseless prey. During the spring, summer, and fall,

75 percent of its diet is made up of mice. The rest is made up of whatever the wolf may find in the way of rabbits, birds, and young or sick animals. Barry Holstun Lopez, in his wonderful book, *Of Wolves and Men*, states that wolves spend one-third of their lives in the pursuit of food and have applied the art of survival in a most impressive way.

In the winter, when the smaller animals go into hibernation, wolves form into packs, numbering as many as twenty in a pack. They hunt animals, such as deer, elk, and moose, that do not hibernate. The packs do not try to capture the strongest of these animals. Instead, they hunt the old, the sick, or the weakened newborns. It is the age old survival of the fittest, God's way of ensuring the perpetuation of the species. Farley Mowat's wonderful book, *Never Cry Wolf*, mentions how for thousands of years these wolves have culled out the weak of a species, thus ensuring its strength and longevity. Like the Eskimos once said, "The wolf is the strength of the elk," for they recognized God's hand in the ways of nature.

Let us examine, for a moment, exactly how wolves exist as hunters. Barry Holstun Lopez made an interesting observation in that regard. It is almost impossible to dislike wolves until you have seen them kill their prey. They are merciless hunters that tear their victims apart, often eating the prey before it has died. Most of their hunting is done at night, seeking out prey that do not see well in the dark. Wolves, by contrast, are blessed with enhanced vision because of a chemical called rodopsin. Not all animals have this, although it is certainly easy to find those that do. The eyes of these animals glow in the dark. I'm sure you have seen a cat's eyes shining on a dark night. That is rodopsin.

Prowling about at night, eyes shining, seeking the weakened prey, and shredding it with powerful jaws. That sounds gruesome, but that is the way wolves have survived. You would expect to name a person or two among those whom wolves have claimed as victims. But that has not happened in this century, nor has it happened on this continent. People have died of rabies as a result of wolf bites, but not strictly from an attack by a wolf. The Indians of Canada and Alaska make claims like this, saying that their history mentions many who died as a result of wolf attacks. Certainly a wolf capable of killing a moose could easily make sport of an average-sized man. Under the right conditions, I have no doubt that a starving wolf would not hesitate to enjoy a "human" meal rather than go without. So let us say that, at the very least, it is not commonplace to hear of any such deadly attacks by wolves.

In the Bible, wolves were often depicted as vicious killers whose hunting capabilities were widely recognized. But they are so much more. Of all animals, wolves stand as perhaps the most outstanding example of devotion to family. Besides being fiercely monogamous, a wolf is the ideal parent, sharing equally with his spouse the responsibility of raising the young. In their immediate families and among their packs, they are loving, loyal, and willing to work together for the common good. Sad how the finer qualities go virtually untold.

There are several Bible verses that speak of the wolves' less likable characteristics. The first is Genesis 49:27. Jacob describes his son Benjamin as a ravenous wolf that in the morning devours its prey. Jeremiah speaks of God's using wolves and other predators to punish His people: "A wolf from the desert will ravage them" (Jer. 5:6). The prophet Ezekiel describes Israel's corrupted officials as being "like wolves tearing their prey" (Ezek. 22:27). Habakkuk describes Israel's long-time enemy Babylon (Iraq) as "fiercer than wolves at dusk" (Hab. 1:8). And Zephaniah calls Israel's corrupt officials "evening wolves, who leave nothing for the morning" (Zeph. 3:3). Yes, most of the Old Testament passages picture wolves as ravenous predators, tearing their prey, and consuming it in the nighttime. The one departure from this consistent image is found in Isaiah. In describing the peaceful kingdom in terms of hunter-and-prey couples, the wolf is the animal that Isaiah twice links with the lamb. (Most people remember this passage incorrectly and associate the lion with the lamb.)

The wolf will live with the lamb.

Isaiah 11:6

The wolf and the lamb will feed together.

Isaiah 65:25

We see in these Scriptures the promise of a complete transformation of the animal's nature. But that is for later. When we will all be changed, when whatever was bad or dangerous about us will be—like the wolves—changed in the twinkling of an eye so that we will not hurt or be hurt anymore. Until that time, there are many things we can learn from the Scriptures to help us withstand the attack of a vicious wolf. The following is a listing of passages from the New Testament. See if you can find in them a formula for wolf proofing your life.

Watch out for false prophets. They come to you in sheep's clothing, but inwardly they are ferocious wolves.

Matthew 7:15

The hired hand is not the shepherd who owns the sheep. So when he sees the wolf coming, he abandons the sheep and runs away. Then the wolf attacks the flock and scatters it.

John 10:12

From these passages, five important elements surface which I believe can be applied to our Christian living. I call them the Rules for Wolf Proofing Your Life.

1. *Watch out for false prophets* (Matt. 7:15). False prophets are everywhere and in different packages. Godless political systems, vain philosophies, and some television evangelists, as interested in your money as

your soul, are the proverbial wolves in sheep's clothing. They are false teachers or teachings, such as the
various cults promote, which represent things that
sound good but are not truthful. If you are not sure of
what you believe, then begin a course of study so that
you do not fall prey to this kind of wolf. After all, it is
difficult to recognize false teaching if you don't know
your own beliefs.

2. *Be wise* (Matt. 10:16). God gives wisdom to
anyone who asks. Life is about making wise choices.
Stay away from wolves like drugs, alcohol, immorality,
crime, unwarranted risks, pornography, lying, and
violence. These can tear your life to pieces. So be
watchful and be wise.

3. *Be innocent* (Matt. 10:16). To be innocent does
not mean to be perfect. It does mean, however, that we
strive to be blameless, that our basic desire must be to
please God. So when we sin, we must quickly repent
and thus remain teachable and humble before God.

God will withdraw his protection from His sheep
who choose to be evil. We can, and sometimes do,
wander off so that we can no longer see the shepherd
or the rest of the flock. It is then that we become vulnerable to the wolves. Being outside the safety of the
flock is to invite trouble.

4. *Don't put your faith in people; trust in Christ* (John
10:12). Jesus is the only one in your life who will never
disappoint you. He is always good. People are not.
Jesus is more than we could begin to hope for and

everything we should strive to be. We are asked to have faith in Jesus—deep, lasting faith. He has earned that from us, and we have every reason to trust Him with even the smallest details of our lives. He will never fail us.

5. *Keep the unity with other believers* (John 10:12). "Then the wolf attacks the flock and scatters it," the passage says. This is the method by which wolves are able to find the weak ones and eliminate them. But standing firm with the Good Shepherd and each other assures our safety.

Remember these five wolf proofers: watchfulness, wisdom, innocence, faith in Christ, and unity with believers.

All of us will have to face wolves of one kind or another. They will try to separate us from our beliefs and from the support of other believers. Just because we are Christians doesn't give us immunity. Be ready, fellow believers, place all your faith in Jesus Christ, and the victory is already won.

11

OSTRICHES

Ostriches are the largest birds in the world, weighing up to three hundred pounds and standing eight feet tall. They are flightless birds, and we thank the Lord for that. They are interesting birds and, as you will see, the Scripture brings them to us without fanfare and without a positive recommendation. Ostriches have very poor credentials.

Little is known about ostriches because their height permits them to see a good way off. They are terrified of humans and run from them with a fierce enthusiasm. A well-known husband-and-wife team, the Sauers, were finally able to observe ostriches by duplicating a termite mound and using it like a hunter's duck blind. Their observations supported what was written about ostriches in the Book of Job more than three thousand years ago.

Ostriches are mentioned in six verses in Job, once in Lamentations, and alluded to in Job 35:11. Only one of these eight verses offers a compliment; the rest are very insulting and focus on ostriches' negative examples. As George Burch, my father-in-law, says, "Everybody is good for something, if only to serve as a bad example."

Let's look at the extended passage in Job:

> The wings of the ostrich wave proudly;
> > but are they the pinions and plumage of
> > love?
> For she leaves her eggs to the earth,
> > and lets them be warmed on the ground,
> forgetting that a foot may crush them,
> > and that the wild beast may trample them.
> She deals cruelly with her young, as if they
> > were not hers;
> > though her labor be in vain, yet she has no
> > fear;
> because God has made her forget wisdom,
> > and given her no share in understanding.
> When she rouses herself to flee,
> > she laughs at the horse and his rider.

Job 39:13–18 RSV

Now count the insults: Verse 13 essentially says that ostriches look good, but looks are deceiving. The Book of Job calls their sincerity into question and suggests that ostriches be evaluated on some basis other than their outward appearance. It's an actions-speak-louder-than-words question that places judgment on the character of the bird. This would have been a good verse for Samson to meditate upon after his first date with Delilah. She was a gorgeous woman, but was she sincere? Her kisses were great, but what was the long view on this relationship? It's obvious that Samson was blind long before the Philistines put out his eyes. Day after day, Delilah proved her insincerity, but Samson was willfully blind to it for no other reason than he didn't want to see it.

We are highly motivated by what we see. That's part of what it means to be human; we're visually oriented. Dogs are motivated by their sense of smell, and black widow spiders are tactile or feeling oriented. Because things are not always as we see them, we need to ask the question, "Is what I'm seeing real?" The Bible commands us to prove all things and hold fast to that which is good. We have permission to avoid getting suckered. We have permission to get the facts. A key factor in the making of wise decisions is to take your time. Time is your friend. Wait and see. Wait until you understand. See how it goes and sift through the information. As it comes to you, evaluate it, weigh its value. Yet even time isn't the perfect criteria for making decisions concerning a person's character. There isn't a perfect criteria. Why? Because evil can lie in wait for long periods of time. This means that no matter how hard we try, some of our decisions concerning a person's character will be wrong. We may not know that for a long time because some evil can be dormant and simply elude the closest scrutiny. Life holds no guarantees. In the case of ostriches, the flaws begin to show up quickly.

In verses 14 and 15, we begin to see these flaws, and they happen to be flaws that most of us hold in great contempt. They are child abuse, child abandonment, child endangerment, and child neglect.

She leaves her eggs to the earth,
(Abandonment)
and lets them be warmed by the ground,
(Neglect)
forgetting that a foot may crush them,
(Abuse)
and that the wild beast may trample them.
(Endangerment)

I found it interesting that ostriches are held in contempt for their lack of mothering skills *before* their babies are born. We're talking about eggs, not young ostriches here. We're talking animals, not people. Do you suppose that God would hold a human mother less responsible for the care of her unborn young than He would an ostrich? Not a chance. In this passage, as in all others, God is pro-life when it comes to unborn young. God is also pro-choice, but He is keenly pro-consequences for our poor choices—our wrongs. Life is sacred, and it begins in the egg for an ostrich. Why should our lives be that different?

I need to let you in on something God knows about the ostrich. If you are an ornithologist, you may already be reacting to this passage because you know why ostriches leave their eggs to the ground to be warmed. The reason is well known. They lay their eggs during a very hot time of the year and incubation is not the issue for them; the issue is air conditioning. They lay down just behind their eggs and fan them to keep them from getting too warm in the ostriches' native desert climate. They're doing fine then, and the earth is the incubating force in the life of the egg. The problem is that ostriches are not careful. Their powerful feet crush their own eggs more often than the hooves of wild beasts.

Ostriches are very apt to wander off and forget what they were doing. That's when the wild beasts get a shot at the eggs. The Egyptian Vulture is a famous enemy of unborn ostriches. It picks up a rock in its beak and slams it against the large egg until it breaks. Then the vulture consumes as much of the egg as it can before hyenas, jackals, or any number of other predators take their shot at this delicacy.

I don't believe that things get any better for ostriches after they're born. Look at verse 16a: "She deals cruelly with her young, as if they were not hers." This really frustrates me about ostriches. When an ostrich family goes out looking for food, the mother will herd the babies ahead of her so that leopards or lions in the area will most likely attack the babies and allow the parents to escape. What kind of mother would do that? But ostriches are not alone as examples of poor parenting. Kangaroos are just as bad, and maybe worse. If a pack of dingo dogs hunts down a mother kangaroo with an infant (a joey) in her pouch, she will pull the infant out and throw it to the dogs. The dogs attack the joey, and the mother escapes.

We get a surprise in verses 16b–17.

> though her labor be in vain, yet she has no
>   fear;
> because God has made her forget wisdom,
>   and given her no share in understanding.

God takes ostriches off the hook. My paraphrase of this verse would read this way: "Even though many of the ostrich's young die because she forgets about them, steps on them, and leaves them to the mercy of horribly violent consequences, she doesn't have to look over her shoulder to see what God is going to do with her. She doesn't have to be afraid of God, because He made her deficient in two ways: she's stupid and she doesn't have a clue."

God is, above all, loving, and an aspect of His love is that He dispenses justice fairly to all of His creation—if not now, later. I am so glad to serve a fair God and to be able to commend Him to others. How horrible it must for atheists who see so few of life's injustices made right. As a Christian, I know that my God is fair and that justice will someday prevail. I know that all wrongs will be made right. I know the good guys will win and the bad guys will lose. Knowing this and believing this comforts me.

Ray Bradbury's writings are an American treasure. Few authors have learned to connect words so elegantly. He weaves marvelous tales of enduring value that offer hope, stimulate thought, teach, and entertain. And his works reflect an optimism that good will triumph over evil. I feel better after reading one of his stories.

Something Wicked This Way Comes is my favorite Bradbury story. The main character of the story, Charles Halloway, must battle against his own fears of aging, death, and inadequacy. He must confront

---

the evil Mr. Dark, who comes to town masquerading as the owner of a carnival. Mr. Dark, however, is much more. He is out to destroy as many lives as he can.

In Charles' first contact with Mr. Dark, he over-hears the sinister Dark whistling a Christmas tune, which is odd to Charles since the story is set in the month of October. The tune has a strange and eerie effect on Charles because it reminds him of two great truths. It makes him think of the words of a hymn:

> I heard the bells on Christmas day
> Their old familiar carols play,
>   And wild and sweet
>   Their words repeat
> Of peace on earth, good will to men!

Charles shivers. Suddenly he feels an old sense of terrified elation, of wanting to laugh and cry at the same time when he sees the innocents of the earth wander the snowy streets on the day before Christmas. The tired men and women have faces dirty with guilt, unwashed of sin, and smashed like small windows by events in their lives that hit without warning, disappear, and come back and hit again.

> Then peeled the bells more loud and deep:
> God is not dead, nor doth he sleep!
>   The Wrong shall fail,
>   The Right prevail,
> With peace on earth, goodwill to men!

At first, we are tempted to see only the injustice, but the volume of the bells increases and leads us to see a deeper truth. Wrong will fail; right will prevail. I have to believe that so I can keep on going. It is part of my incentive to serve God. God is fair and there is no one else to appeal to for justice. He is the only one.

Ostriches offer us hope. God will not hold us accountable to be something we can't be. If God has not given us the power or the ability to accomplish something, we will not be held accountable for it anymore than witless, clueless ostriches are held accountable for their failures at mothering.

On the other hand, we are accountable for what we can do and have been gifted to do. As far as parenting is concerned, all but a few can understand that. Ostriches abandon, neglect, abuse, and endanger their young; they are the antithesis of God's ideal for parenting. He would have us remember that we have four tasks as parents.

1. We must take responsibility for our young, meaning that parents need to spend time with their children or provide for loving care. Television and the streets are raising too many children these days.

2. We must nurture and care for our children, meeting their basic needs for food, shelter, clothing, and education. We need to prepare them for life.

3. We must love our children, which covers everything from encouragement, hugs, and kisses to discipline and character development.

4. We must protect our children from their own immaturity and also from what is out there these days. Today, life is filled with dragons.

Parenting is a full-time job that most people are attempting to accomplish part time. If we parent like an ostrich, most of us are going to hear about it. Think about this: If we neglect our children like ostriches neglect theirs, we'll get little, selfish, neglectful, abusive creatures lacking in wisdom and understanding.

The Scripture ends on a positive note concerning the ostrich, however. And for that, I am glad for them.

> When she rouses herself to flee,
>   she laughs at the horse and his rider.

Horses mentioned in the Bible were most likely Arabians. They are elegant pictures of grace when they run. Arabians have been clocked at thirty-five miles an hour when they run flat out; their riders feel like the wind. But ostriches can run forty-five miles an hour. As elegant as an Arabian stallion might be, a three-hundred-pound bird can lose him.

A summary of this passage would say that ostriches are lousy mothers, but boy, can they run. In context, God is saying to Job, "When you look at life, there are many things you can't understand. Why I made the ostrich the way I did is one of those things. I have my reasons, and I'm not going to let you in on all of them. I also have my reasons for allowing your suffering, and I'm not going to tell you those either. Just trust Me!"

12

Locusts

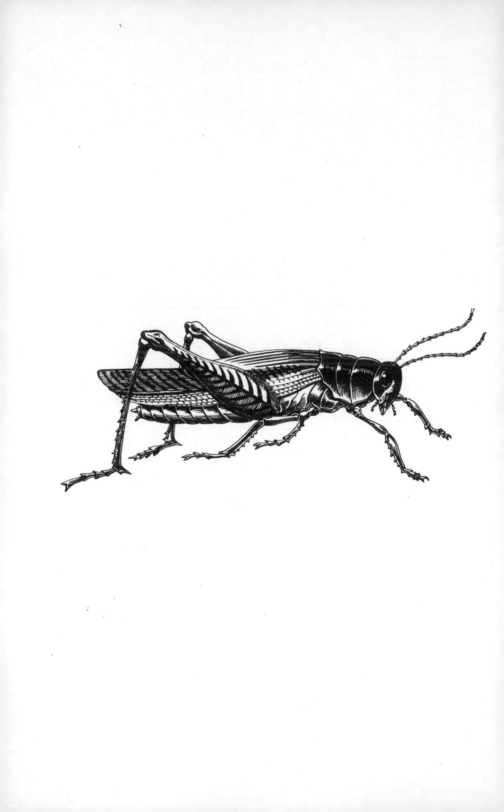

Locusts ARE MENTIONED FAR more times than all the other insects of the Bible combined. They have three characteristics. In Proverbs 30, they represent unity. In Exodus 10, they are pictured as destroyers, which is the dominant meaning given to them throughout the passages in which they are mentioned. In Leviticus 11, they are food. Locusts were the only insect food that the children of Israel were allowed to eat (Lev. 11:22). In fact, they are still eaten in the Middle East today.

Let's look at some of the passages in which they appear.

> The locusts have no king,
> yet all of them march in rank.
>
> *Proverbs 30:27 RSV*

In Proverbs, Solomon allows Agur, his naturalist friend, an opportunity to teach through nature. Solomon's father, David, was an outdoorsman, but Solomon didn't spend much time in nature. Because he was a rich kid and grew up around the palace rather than around the sheepfold and pasture, Agur speaks for him at this point. This verse is one of four under the heading, "Four things on earth are small, but they are exceedingly wise."

Agur noticed that although locusts have no leadership, they do have a unity of purpose. When locusts swarm, they go in the same direction and do the same thing, accomplishing a common goal without any leadership.

Locusts don't accomplish much beyond survival, which means that they eat. They like to eat banquet style. When locusts swarm, they do it in a big way. Desmond Morris in his wonderful book, *Animal Watching*, tells us that the average swarm of locusts is made up of 40 billion individuals who eat 40 million pounds of food a day. The largest recorded swarm was two thousand miles long and had an estimated population of 250 billion locusts. They would have eaten 250 million pounds of food a day. Food is vegetation, the vegetation that we eat. They are devastating when they unify.

Unity is wise. Big things are accomplished by working together. And the Lord loves it when His saints dwell together in love. That's why He gave us this picture of unity. We don't need a human king to accomplish what we were made for. If we just stuck to our purpose to love and to serve God, we would accomplish our goal. We know that locusts are simply being obedient to God when they march. They have little control over their flight; they go where the wind takes them. They go where they are led and do what they were made to do. Wouldn't it be great if we were as simply directed? But God has made us free moral agents, and unity of purpose is something we arrive at with a willing spirit and a common vision. With our fallen natures we don't opt for unity very often, so we often see very little accomplished. When the wind of God's spirit blows hard among His people, there have been revivals. That is when we see great things done for God by His power.

I saw the Jesus People movement of the 1960s and 1970s and hope to live long enough to see another revival like it. During that time, there was a clear perception of people's need for Christ, an awareness of our sin and need for grace. People knew they needed to study God's word and worship. There was unity and much was accomplished during that period. Much of that good is slipping away now and being replaced by a movement to help people feel better. The church is going in so many directions to meet such a diversity of needs it has lost its mass unity of purpose, its focus. By God's grace it can come back.

The usual context in which the locust is found is the context of destruction. The destruction is either against Israel's enemies to assist Israel or against Israel for turning its back on God. In Exodus 10 we see God lashing out against Egypt, using locusts as an awful agent of destruction.

The locusts were the eighth of ten mighty plagues that God used to demonstrate His awesome power. Before the plague of locusts, the Nile had been turned to blood and the land had been filled with frogs. Moses had filled the air of Egypt with gnats, and then the Lord cranked it up a notch and filled the land with flies. Then God caused all the Egyptian cattle to die. Things got really ugly when God caused boils to form over every Egyptian male and over any livestock owned by an Egyptian. God then sent hail and fire to rain down upon the people. It destroyed most of their crops. That's when the locusts came.

It is worth asking the question why God did all these incredible things. There are many reasons. First, He wanted to establish Moses' credibility. Second, He wanted to build morale in His people, because they had been beaten down by years of slavery and cruelty. Third, He wanted to demonstrate the absolute impotence of the Egyptian gods. Fourth, He wanted to demonstrate His fierce love and loyalty to His chosen people by answering their prayer for deliverance. Fifth, and perhaps most important, He was establishing for all time that He was God, the only true God, and there wasn't anything He couldn't do if He willed to do it. Finally, God was giving the Egyptians a chance to come to Him, but they never did.

The plague of locusts was really impressive, as were the plagues that preceded it. This story reads like this:

> And the LORD said to Moses, "Stretch out your hand over Egypt so that locusts will swarm over the land and devour everything growing in the fields, everything left by the hail."

So Moses stretched out his staff over Egypt, and the LORD made an east wind blow across the land all that day and all that night. By morning the wind had brought the locusts; they invaded all Egypt and settled down in every area of the country in great numbers. Never before had there been such a plague of locusts, nor will there ever be again. They covered all the ground until it was black. They devoured all that was left after the hail—everything growing in the fields and the fruit on the trees. Nothing green remained on tree or plant in all the land of Egypt.

Pharaoh quickly summoned Moses and Aaron and said, "I have sinned against the LORD your God and against you. Now forgive my sin once more and pray to the LORD your God to take this deadly plague away from me."

Moses then left Pharaoh and prayed to the LORD. And the LORD changed the wind to a very strong west wind, which caught up the locusts and carried them into the Red Sea. Not a locust was left anywhere in Egypt. But the LORD hardened Pharaoh's heart, and he would not let the Israelites go.

Exodus 10:12–20

Egypt is about 600 miles long and about 600 wide. That means that God blew in enough locusts to cover every square inch of a country that has 360,000 square miles of land. Talk about defoliation! Over 360,000 square miles of wall-to-wall locusts could do it to you. Not one green plant was left in all the land of Egypt. The ground was black with locusts. They ate everything that the hail had not destroyed. Egypt is mostly desert, but the Nile River Delta is a wonderful farming area—although not that year.

Frankly there was nothing to eat anywhere, except locusts, which are 80 percent protein and 20 percent carbohydrates and chocked full of every vitamin and mineral imaginable. John the Baptist's diet was mostly locusts and wild honey (Matt. 3:4), and he did just fine. Locusts could be dried and made into flour. Given the number of locusts in this plague, the Egyptians would have had plenty to eat for a long, long time. Yet their Pharaoh was not a big-league decision-maker. Pharaoh had allowed his country to be dismantled completely by God in much the same way that Saddam Hussein allowed Iraq to be dismantled by the United Nations coalition. Pharaoh asked Moses to pray to God to remove the locusts. Pharaoh forgot they didn't have any more food. They had some stored grain, but not enough to avoid a famine of catastrophic proportions.

God did an interesting thing. He created a strong west wind that blew the billions of locusts into the Red Sea. The fish must have been ecstatic. I think the Lord was being gracious to the Egyptians despite their lame leader. With an increased food supply for the fish, there would have been a yield of fish beyond anything they could have hoped for. The decimation of their land was complete, and I'm sure they would have had to lean heavily on the sea to survive the next several years. The surrounding countries probably did a big grain business off of Egypt for a while also. The world had never seen a plague of locusts like that and never will again.

Many centuries after their deliverance from Egypt, Israel turned from God, and God chose to send a mighty plague of locusts on them in response to their rebellion. It is as if the Lord were saying, "I can do to you exactly what I did to the Egyptians. I could handle their rebellion, and I can handle yours." It was a severe punishment to Israel; the Lord must have wanted it to be remembered for generations:

> The word of the LORD that came to Joel, the son of Pethuel:
>
> Hear this, you aged men,
>   give ear, all inhabitants of the land!
> Has such a thing happened in your days,
>   or in the days of your fathers?
> Tell your children of it,
>   and let your children tell their children,
>   and their children another generation.
>
> What the cutting locust left,
>   the swarming locust has eaten.
> What the swarming locust left,
>   the hopping locust has eaten,
> and what the hopping locust left,
>   the destroying locust has eaten.

Joel 1:1–4 RSV

The plague of locusts had one purpose only: to turn the people back to God. There are times when God has to take even the things we really need to bring us back to what we need most. We need God,

and we need Him even more than we need food.
When we are doing fine, there is a great temptation to
simply set Him aside and rely on our own resources.
But we were not created to rely on our own resources.
We were created to love and to serve God; He will do
what He needs to do to see that His people do just
that—love Him and serve Him.

In Joel 2, we see just what happens when the
people repented and returned to the Lord. It's wonderful.

> Fear not, O land;
>   be glad and rejoice,
>   for the LORD has done great things!
> Fear not, you beasts of the field,
>   for the pastures of the wilderness are green;
>   the tree bears its fruit,
>   the fig tree and vine give their full yield.
> Be glad, O sons of Zion,
>   and rejoice in the LORD, your God;
> for he has given the early rain for your vindi-
>   cation,
>   he has poured down for you abundant rain,
>   the early and the latter rain, as before.
> The threshing floors shall be full of grain,
>   the vats shall overflow with wine and oil.
> I will restore to you the years
>   which the swarming locust has eaten,
> the hopper, the destroyer, and the cutter,
>   my great army, which I sent among you.

>   *Joel 2:21–25* RSV

This is a wonderful grace that God promises to His children only: I will restore to you the years that the locusts have eaten. He doesn't restore the years because we deserve them. When we have been disobedient, we don't deserve blessing, restoration, or reward. It is His grace. When we return to Him, He has achieved His end. Discipline and grace seem to be two of the tools that God uses to mold our lives. Devastation is not one of the tools that He uses on His beloved children. He will give us a good spanking when we need it, then, when it has had its proper effect, we are restored, established, and strengthened.

I remember that my father spanked me a lot. I earned those spankings, every one of them. Spankings and punishments were not fun when they were happening, but they were always followed up with love, forgiveness, and the restoration of fellowship. Those things always made up for the lost privileges, the brief pain, the loss of approval, and the break in fellowship. I know just what God was saying when He said that He would restore to His people the years of the locust. Our years of the locust are the years that have to happen to bring us to the point where God's love is again important to us. Those years make clear our need for God. If God didn't love me, He would either destroy me or walk away from me when I get out of line. As it stands, God goes to a lot of trouble to keep His children well behaved. I am glad that He does.

13

HORSES

Horses are, beyond a shadow of a doubt, the most admired, valued, and coveted animals on the earth. They are the most often reproduced animal by artists, for horses are truly in and of themselves works of art. For thousands of years, horses have been partners in man's most costly work, serving both as transportation and as tools. The agricultural and industrial revolutions of Western civilization were supported and strengthened by the services of these fine animals, whose contributions are immeasurable.

In Bible times, a horse's purpose was especially significant. These animals were the principle means of personal transportation for the wealthy. They were used in battle because they could be trained to trust their riders and work with them against an enemy. Horses were also used to pull chariots into battle. And they were raced. For years, horse racing has been referred to as the sport of kings.

Of all animals, horses are the most noble in appearance, rivaled only, but not excelled, by male lions with full manes. Jesus Himself chooses to ride a horse into the last great battle, where He will defeat two beings of incredible evil and slay their followers. This white horse, I believe, although I cannot prove, will be the finest Arabian that has ever been seen. Arabians are both extremely beautiful and well known for their incredible endurance. They are the oldest breed and have been the pride of the Middle East for thousands of years. It just seems logical that as a reward for faithful service, an Arabian would be chosen to bear the King of kings into His final triumph. It is worth reading that section of Scripture where these things are revealed. It is found in the Book of the Revelation:

Then I saw heaven opened, and there was a white horse! Its rider is called Faithful and True, and in righteousness he judges and makes war. His eyes are like a flame of fire, and on his head are many diadems; and he has a name inscribed that no one knows but himself. He is clothed in a robe dipped in blood, and his name is called The Word of God. And the armies of heaven, wearing fine linen, white and pure, were following him on white horses. From his mouth comes a sharp sword with which to strike down the nations, and he will rule them with a rod of iron; he will tread the winepress of the fury of the wrath of God the Almighty. On his robe and on his thigh he has a name inscribed, "King of kings and Lord of lords."

Then I saw an angel standing in the sun, and with a loud voice he called to all the birds that fly in midheaven, "Come, gather for the great supper of God, to eat the flesh of kings, the flesh of captains, the flesh of the mighty, the flesh of horses and their riders—flesh of all, both free and slave, both small and great." Then I saw the beast and the kings of the earth with their armies gathered to make war against the rider on the horse and against his army. And the beast was captured, and with it the false prophet who had performed in its presence the signs by which he had deceived those who had received the mark of the beast and those who worshiped its image. These two were thrown alive into the lake of fire that burns with sulfur. And the rest were killed by the sword of the rider on the horse, the sword that came from his mouth; and all the birds were gorged with their flesh.

Revelation 19:11–21 NRSV

Earlier, in the Book of the Revelation, we are given a glimpse of Christ as the conquering king on a white horse. It is not as detailed but is still impressive and regal.

I looked, and there was a white horse! Its rider had a bow; a crown was given to him, and he came out conquering and to conquer.

Revelation 6:2 NRSV

Although Revelation contains the most majestic use of a horse, I also enjoy the part a horse plays in a story from the Old Testament. In the Book of Esther there is a villain you love to hate. His name is Haman. He rises to power and is second only to the mighty King Ahasuerus (most likely King Xerxes). Haman is conceited. He is also cruel. He is pompous "to the max" and prejudiced against the Jews because they will not worship him like a god.

Along comes Mordecai, the real hero of the story. He is a godly man and a Jewish slave who manages to get on Haman's bad side because he will not bow down and worship him. Mordecai worships the God of heaven and only Him. In recompense, Haman decides that all the Jews must die, thousands of them. He arranges the atrocity by tricking the king into signing an irreversible edict that will make it so. Meanwhile, Mordecai has already established his loyalty to the king by having revealed an assassination plot, a timely bit of news that saves the king's life. The heroic deed is recorded in the king's diary, but, unfortunately, he forgets to give Mordecai his just reward. Well, just about the time Haman is ready to have Mordecai and all the Jews killed, the king remembers that he has not done anything to thank Mordecai for saving his life. Even at this point the king has no idea that Haman has tricked him into signing the death warrant for all Jews, including Mordecai and the king's beautiful wife Esther (who, at Mordecai's insistence, has never made it known that she, too, is Jewish).

One sleepless night, while having a servant reread a selection from his personal journal, the king is reminded of his debt to Mordecai. The next morning, he sends for Haman to advise him concerning the reward for Mordecai's honorable deed. This is what happens:

Now Haman had just entered the outer court of the king's palace to speak to the king about having

Mordecai hanged on the gallows that he had prepared for him. So the king's servants told him, "Haman is there, standing in the court." The king said, "Let him come in." So Haman came in, and the king said to him, "What shall be done for the man whom the king wishes to honor?" Haman said to himself, "Whom would the king wish to honor more than me?" So Haman said to the king, "For the man whom the king wishes to honor, let royal robes be brought, which the king has worn, and a horse that the king has ridden, with a royal crown on its head. Let the robes and the horse be handed over to one of the king's most noble officials; let him robe the man whom the king wishes to honor, and let him conduct the man on horseback through the open square of the city, proclaiming before him: 'Thus shall it be done for the man whom the king wishes to honor.'" Then the king said to Haman, "Quickly, take the robes and the horse, as you have said, and do so to the Jew Mordecai who sits at the king's gate. Leave out nothing you have mentioned." So Haman took the robes and the horse and robed Mordecai and led him riding through the open square of the city, proclaiming, "Thus shall it be done to the man whom the king wishes to honor."

Esther 6:4–11 NRSV

It was downhill for Haman after that. When the king found out that Haman had brought him into a plot that would have brought about the death of his beloved and beautiful queen, he had Haman killed— hanged on the very gallows Haman had constructed for Mordecai. In fact, he had Haman's whole family killed. But that's the way kings did things in those days. Kings didn't like the idea of any angry family member lurking about, seeking revenge for dad's death. This method was very effective in preventing assassinations.

Did you notice that of all possible honors that might have been bestowed upon him, riding the king's horse was virtually at the top of the list. You can bet Mordecai enjoyed every moment of that ride. Perhaps there is a beautiful white horse awaiting each of us in the army of the Lord. Being children of His royal kingdom, we may just have a royal surprise of that nature awaiting us. (It's either that, or a Mercedes, I think.)

I am reminded of the motion picture *The Black Stallion*, one of the best films of recent years. The proud and noble steed is the embodiment of a lineage that is fearfully and wonderfully made. He can run like the wind; he is brave, strong, and spirited. Isn't it exciting to know that we, like the tribe of Judah as described in Zechariah, are being groomed to receive God's blessing and gifts. Read from the tenth chapter:

> My anger is hot against the shepherds,
>   and I will punish the leaders;
> for the LORD of hosts cares for his flock, and
> the house of Judah,
>   and will make them like his proud war
> horse in battle.
>
> *Zechariah 10:3* NRSV

We belong to God and His promises are ours. When we are right with God, we can hold our heads high. When we are right with God, we stand trembling with excitement to serve Him. When we are right with God, we see that our causes are noble ones. When we are right with God, we do not let our fears paralyze us. Just like the tribe of Judah, nothing will be denied us who proudly follow the Lord our God. Think noble!

Horses are really a remarkable creation and one that God takes rightful pride in having made. Like the majestic black stallion, like the proud steed that God would have us become, we go about our lives in ready anticipation, prepared to face the unknown.

> Who led them through the depths?
> Like a horse in the desert,
>   they did not stumble.
>
> *Isaiah 63:13* NRSV

Horses, by their very existence, are wondrous reminders that God is there and is not silent. He speaks volumes from the beauty of His creation. Just look at a beautiful horse and try not to be impressed. Impossible!

14

DONKEYS

Donkeys are relatively small, useful animals. They were the chief farming animals of peasant farmers and were also used for plowing on smaller farms when oxen were not cost-efficient. In modern terms, donkeys were the pick-up trucks of the ancient world.

The Book of Numbers contains one of the most fascinating animal stories in all of Scripture, and its most memorable character is a donkey. It is part of the chronicle of the people of Israel and their march from Egypt to the Promised Land. The Exodus took them across several countries, and the people they encountered along the way didn't always believe that these twelve tribes were just passing through. Moses sent messengers out to ask for safe passage for the people. The first to be contacted, Sihon king of the Amorites, not only refused to permit the Hebrews to use the "interstate," he gathered his entire army and attacked the people in the desert. Bad move. The Lord took care of Sihon and his troops, and Israel took over the lands of the Amorites.

A neighboring king, Og of Bashan, didn't waste any time in challenging this new people. He took his army to meet Israel at a place known as Endrei. And the Bible says that the Lord told Moses not to worry. He said, "I have handed him over to you. . . . Do to him what you did to Sihon." And Israel added Bashan to their newly acquired holdings.

Needless to say, this spooked the other people in the area. Balak king of Moab was afraid that he was next. So he met with the rulers of the neighboring kingdom of Midian, and they decided to contact the area holy man. Balak and his friends figured that Israel had a kind of special magic that made them invincible. In a way they were right, because the Lord was over-seeing the whole thing. But to Balak it seemed logical to counter this spiritual power with another spiritual power, one that he could control. So he sent for Balaam, the regional prophet, saying, "A people has come out of Egypt; they cover the face of the land and have settled next to me. Now come and put a curse on these people, because they are too powerful for me. Perhaps then I will be able to defeat them and drive them out of the country. For I know that those you bless are blessed, and those you curse are cursed."

What Balak didn't realize was that Balaam knew the Lord. When his people contacted Balaam, Balaam asked the Lord if he should take the contract. The Lord said no. So Balaam said no. Balak countered by saying that he could make it more profitable for the prophet but he was coming one way or another, either on his donkey or tied to its back. When Balaam then asked the Lord what he should do, the Lord told him to go,

---

but he should speak only what the Lord wanted him to say. Let's pick the story up there:

Balaam got up in the morning, saddled his donkey and went with the princes of Moab. But God was very angry when he went, and the angel of the Lord stood in the road to oppose him. Balaam was riding on his donkey, and his two servants were with him. When the donkey saw the angel of the Lord standing in the road with a drawn sword in his hand, she turned off the road into a field. Balaam beat her to get her back on the road.

Then the angel of the Lord stood in a narrow path between two vineyards, with walls on both sides. When the donkey saw the angel of the Lord, she pressed close to the wall, crushing Balaam's foot against it. So he beat her again.

Then the angel of the Lord moved on ahead and stood in a narrow place where there was no room to turn, either to the right or to the left. When the donkey saw the angel of the Lord, she lay down under Balaam, and he was angry and beat her with his staff. Then the Lord opened the donkey's mouth, and she said to Balaam, "What have I done to you to make you beat me these three times?"

Balaam answered the donkey, "You have made a fool of me! If I had a sword in my hand, I would kill you right now."

The donkey said to Balaam, "Am I not your own donkey, which you have always ridden, to this day? Have I been in the habit of doing this to you?"

"No," he said.

> Then the Lord opened Balaam's eyes, and he saw the angel of the Lord standing in the road with his sword drawn. So he bowed low and fell facedown."
>
> *Numbers 22:21–35*

In the exchange that follows between Balaam and the angel, the man repents of his sin and says that if the Lord doesn't want him to meet up with Balak, he won't. The angel, however, instructs him to go on, but he reminds Balaam to only say what the Lord directs him to say. As a result, Balaam pronounces seven blessings on Israel (Num. 23:1–24:24), and Balak is frustrated and returns home.

I've read that story again and again. The first time I was fascinated by the talking donkey and the power of God to give speech to an animal. But then I got to thinking about Balaam. He doesn't act a bit surprised that his donkey can talk. They chat as amiably as Wilbur and Mr. Ed. Now either Balaam and his donkey had a long history of conversations behind them, or Balaam realized that the Lord had decided to use his animal as a way of straightening him out. After all, if your donkey can see the angel of the Lord when you can't, then you need a lot of straightening out.

So what was the problem? Balaam was only doing what the Lord had told him to do. Then why was the angel of the Lord blocking the road, and why was his sword drawn? I think we get close to answering both questions when we look at Numbers 22:18 and 24:13. Twice Balaam refers to his fee for coming to Balak; he claims he can only say what the Lord would have him say "even if Balak gave me his palace filled with silver and gold." Something tells me that Balaam was trying as hard as he could to follow the Lord, but if he cursed the people of Israel in Balak's name, he'd have a handsome fortune to show for it. With that kind of profit margin, he could retire, right?

I think Balaam's ponderings of wealth and what it could buy preoccupied him as he rode his little donkey to the rendezvous with Balak. The Lord sent his angel to remind Balaam to whom he should show his loyalty, but the Lord's prophet couldn't see this messenger for his daydreaming about the gold and silver that would be his. Nothing was definite. The Lord could tell him to curse this new people . . .

While wealth filled Balaam's mind, death confronted his seeing-eye donkey. Even after the first two donkey maneuvers, Balaam didn't yet see the danger before him. The third time, however, the donkey spoke, Balaam saw, and the heavenly messenger cleared the prophet's mind of his fanciful golden dreams. The Lord had used a simple beast of burden to get His prophet to hear His voice over the din of the clatter of coins. It took the voice of a donkey to grab Balaam's attention and focus it on the Lord's will. And from the enlightenment given by the donkey, the Lord's people were blessed.

The donkey reminded Balaam about her constant faithfulness to him, and that reflected a faithfulness that he needed to remember toward the Lord. She

must have been a charming, faithful little animal.
When I get to heaven, I hope to find that Balaam cher-
ished her faithfulness beyond the intersection of Balak
Boulevard and Angel Avenue.

Anything can happen with the Lord. Sometimes
we're blinded by our own desires and miss the things
that donkey-vision never misses. When that happens,
let's hope that the Lord has a talking donkey nearby
and that we have the ears to hear even when we lack
the eyes to see.

My favorite New Testament donkey is the one
Jesus rode into Jerusalem on Palm Sunday. This simple
act spoke volumes about how Jesus wanted the people
to see Him. Keep in mind that the people wanted a
warrior king to drive the Romans out of the land and
set up a powerful Jewish country and maybe even a
worldwide empire. This is who the Messiah was supposed to be. All the prophets had written about the
retribution that was due to the nations whom the Lord
had allowed to punish Israel for disobeying Him. But
surely that time was past. Surely Israel had atoned.
Surely the Lord had forgiven. Now was the time of the
Messiah. He would gather his own legions and push
the Romans into the sea. That had to be the divine
plan. Or so most people thought.

And everyone knew what Jesus was doing. He
preached repentance and said a lot about love of God
and love for each other. But you know politicians.
They'll say anything or do anything to get some support. This Jesus, though, was doing some powerful

stuff. All those healings. He was powerful, no doubt about it. And He was religious. He fit the profile.

So when the word spread that Jesus was coming to Jerusalem, a lot of people concluded that He was ready to make His move. It was particularly important that He was coming to Jerusalem at Passover. There was no more important holiday than that on the Jewish calendar. And just as that celebration represented the Lord's deliverance of His people from one oppressor, this could be the beginning of a new deliverance.

Everyone lined the entry route to Jerusalem hoping to be among the first to see the Messiah and His twelve lieutenants. No scene was better set for the arrival of a new general. George Armstrong Custer would have given most anything for this moment. A flourish of trumpets, the clatter of horse hooves, the thunderous entrance of a new leader.

Didn't happen. Instead, the Messiah came on a donkey.

Donkeys didn't carry great warriors into battle. Donkeys didn't pull war chariots in and out of the Valley of the Shadow of Death. Donkeys were . . . peaceful. They were quiet creatures that only made noise if they didn't want to do something. Sometimes they were stubborn animals, but they were also dependable and almost tireless beasts capable of carrying heavier burdens than horses farther than horses.

Whereas most people pictured their rulers on horseback, in the ancient near east kings and princes also rode donkeys. The difference between the two usually related to the state of affairs in the land. A horse-riding king was a warrior; a donkey-riding monarch surveyed a peaceful land from his saddle. The former meted out justice with a sword; the latter pronounced justice with his words.

So Jesus' entry on a donkey said in so many words, "I am the Messiah, but I am not a warrior to fight your imagined battles. I come in peace as a servant king, emphasizing my servant's heart, and setting an example for you to have servant hearts." The following is Matthew's account of the triumphal entry of Jesus into Jerusalem:

> As they approached Jerusalem and came to Bethphage on the Mount of Olives, Jesus sent two disciples, saying to them, "Go to the village ahead of you, and at once you will find a donkey tied there, with her colt by her. Untie them and bring them to me. If anyone says anything to you, tell him that the Lord needs them, and he will send them right away."
>
> This took place to fulfill what was spoken through the prophet: .
>
> > "Say to the daughter of Zion,
> > 'See, your king comes to you,
> > gentle and riding on a donkey,
> > on a colt, the foal of a donkey.'"
>
> The disciples went and did as Jesus had instructed them. They brought the donkey and the colt, placed their cloaks on them, and Jesus sat on them. A very large crowd spread their cloaks on the road,

---

while others cut branches from the trees and spread them on the road. The crowds that went ahead of him and those that followed shouted,

> "Hosanna to the son of David!"
> "Blessed is he who comes in the name of the Lord!"
> "Hosanna in the highest!"

> When Jesus entered Jerusalem, the whole city was stirred and asked, "Who is this?"
> The crowds answered, "This is Jesus, the prophet from Nazareth in Galilee."

Matthew 21:1–11

This was the very first time Jesus allowed the people to treat Him as a king, and He chose a peaceful animal known for it servileness to convey the meaning of His kingship to the people. Through the donkey, Jesus made clear that He had come to serve and not to be served. And the message for those who follow Him is that we too are to serve as faithfully as the donkey serves his master. We may bray out of our own stubbornness from time to time, but we know that there is no greater honor than that we journey with the Lord, humble, ready servants, carrying our King into the hearts of those around us.